THE CLIENT-CENTRED THERAPIST IN PSYCHIATRIC CONTEXTS

A THERAPISTS' GUIDE TO THE PSYCHIATRIC LANDSCAPE AND ITS INHABITANTS

THE CLIENT-CENTRED THERAPIST IN PSYCHIATRIC CONTEXTS

A THERAPISTS' GUIDE TO THE PSYCHIATRIC LANDSCAPE AND ITS INHABITANTS

LISBETH SOMMERBECK

PCCS BOOKS
Ross-on-Wye

First published in 2003

PCCS BOOKS
Llangarron
Ross-on-Wye
Herefordshire
HR9 6PT
UK
Tel +44 (0)1989 77 07 07
enquiries@pccsbks.globalnet.co.uk
www.pccs-books.co.uk

**The Client-Centred Therapist in Psychiatric Contexts
A therapists' guide to the psychiatric landscape and its
inhabitants**

British Library Cataloguing in Publication Data.
A catalogue record for this book is available from the British Library.

ISBN 1 898059 55 1

Cover design by Old Dog Graphics
Printed by Bookcraft, Midsomer Norton, UK

CONTENTS

ACKNOWLEDGEMENTS

Among the participants in the discussions on the e-mail networks[1] coordinated by Marco Temaner and Jerold Bozarth, I am particularly indebted to Garry Prouty, John Shlien, Barbara Brodley and Marvin Frankel. I am deeply grateful for the interest they took in discussing the ideas of this book with me.

Garry Prouty also took the time to review the manuscript. His enthusiasm about it strengthened my confidence in it, and his comments helped me clarify some of my ideas in a more coherent and systematic way. It was also a relief to know that he found my presentation of Pre-therapy loyal to his thinking.

John Shlien offered to review the manuscript, an offer I, of course, gratefully accepted. However, it wasn't to be. Shortly after I had sent the manuscript to him, the news of his death reached me. I still miss him.

Barbara Brodley has been my main support. Right from the start of our correspondence she found my ideas worth listening and responding to, inspiring me to think, and slowly to trust, that what I had in mind might be useful to others.

Marvin Frankel has been my main challenge. By his generous sharing of his own ideas and his sensitive and inspiring questioning of major points of confusion in my thinking I have reached a place where my understanding of the theory of client-centred therapy and my daily practice makes sense to me as a unified whole.

1. Lists dedicated to Client-Centred Therapy and the Person-Centred Approach. You can join the cctpca network by sending a blank email to <cctpca-join@texaslists.net> or to join PCINTNL (PCA theory-oriented) send an email asking to join to <jbozarth1@charter.net>.

DEDICATION

I'd like to dedicate this book to all the participants in the discussions on the cctpca networks coordinated by Marco Temaner and Jerold Bozarth. Without this opportunity to discuss my ideas, the present book would never have come into existence.

INTRODUCTION

THE PSYCHIATRIC LANDSCAPE AND ITS INHABITANTS

The psychiatric landscape is vast and varied. There are psychiatric hospitals, psychiatric wards in general hospitals, day hospitals, outpatient or community clinics, GP consultations, home services, activity centres, sheltered living facilities, sheltered day care, occupational and educational facilities, etc., in all shapes and variations.

In this book, I intend the terms 'psychiatric context', 'medical model setting' and 'psychiatric setting', which are used interchangeably, to be understood broadly. Whenever a client-centred therapist interacts with a person who also receives some kind of medical service or psychiatric service to effect some kind of psychological change in him, that same therapist is working with or within a medical model context or psychiatric context. He interacts with a person who has a psychiatric diagnosis. This is the case whether the person is simply taking some psychopharmacological medicine prescribed by a GP, whom the therapist has never seen and never will see, or whether the person is an in-patient in a psychiatric hospital. Within these two extremes, there are persons using one or several of the other psychiatric services mentioned above. Although this book is written from within the context of a psychiatric hospital, much of it should be easily applicable to other, less extreme, psychiatric contexts.

The inhabitants of the psychiatric landscape are correspondingly numerous and varied. There are two major groups of inhabitants. One group comprises the professionals, i.e. all the employees or staff members: psychiatrists, nurses, social workers, psychologists, occupational therapists, physiotherapists, and many others. Included in this group is the very rare client-centred therapist. Staff members ordinarily define themselves as precisely that: staff members. Such is not the case with the other major group of inhabitants, those who are ordinarily defined as patients. Among this group are a small number of persons who do not regard themselves as patients. They either see themselves as prisoners of psychiatry, or they do not define themselves with respect to psychiatry at all. They have been involuntarily committed to psychiatric treatment, most often in a closed ward, either actively resisting or passively following. They are regarded by staff members as being, in some way or another, dangerous to, or threatening the health of, themselves and/or others on the basis of a psychotic condition. National legislation in most countries obliges staff members, and gives them the right, to treat these people 'for their own sake'.

By far the majority of patients, though, define themselves as patients. I shall therefore, for the sake of easy reading, use this term in the book, without constantly reminding the reader that some patients do not define themselves as such. There are inhabitants in the psychiatric landscape whose only expressed wish is to leave it, or who express neither any wish to be there, nor any wish to leave.

Those persons I have termed 'clients' are persons who define themselves as psychiatric patients and, in addition, actively seek and receive psychotherapy. I shall, however, also describe how a client-centred therapist can interact in a person-centred way with other patients who do not actively define themselves as clients, and with staff members. I shall sometimes use the term 'person-centred practice' to designate this kind of interaction, and I shall explain what I see as the major difference between my person-centred practice, on the one hand, and my client-centred therapy practice, on the other. Whether I'm describing one or the other, however, I shall retain the term 'client-centred therapist', although the term 'person-centred practitioner' might sometimes be more appropriate. This, too, is done for the sake of easy reading.

I prefer the term 'client-centred therapy' to the term 'person-centred therapy' because I think the more traditional term accepts and respects the client's definition of himself as precisely that: a client. When a person turns to a therapist for help, he hopes that the therapist will interact with him in a way that is as therapeutically beneficial to him as possible, and that the therapist will consistently have this as his first priority. He does not seek out a therapist in order that the therapist will interact with him in the way the therapist interacts with friends, colleagues, relatives, and other persons in general. In short, he defines himself as a client, and I want to respect that by using the terms 'client-centred therapist' and 'client-centred therapy'.

In addition, I have chosen, again for the sake of easy reading, to use the traditional application of pronouns: he, him and his. The inhabitants of the psychiatric landscape are, of course, made up of both sexes, and to those who may feel offended by my choice, seeing it as an expression of sexual discrimination, I apologise.

Finally, a group of patients who will not be mentioned in this book are children. The reason is, quite simply, that I have no experience of client-centred therapy with children, and no experience with children in psychiatric contexts.

Although my practice differs somewhat according to my distinction between my person-centred practice with the inhabitants of the psychiatric landscape who do not define themselves as clients, and my client-centred therapy practice with those who do define themselves as clients, the organisation of this book does not correspond to this differentiation of my work. Rather, apart from a description of the therapist's person-centred interaction with other staff members, it corresponds to three broad, traditional, diagnostic categories of psychiatry ('psychotically depressed', 'psychotic', 'near-psychotic'), because they pose the more characteristic challenges to the client-centred therapist working within a psychiatric context.

It is at the heart of the philosophy of client-centred therapy to see diagnoses (and the process of diagnosing, within a psychotherapeutic setting) as discriminatory, and at variance with the therapist's unconditional positive regard and empathic understanding, which are assumed to be the therapeutic factors in client-centred therapy. Psychiatric diagnoses are not an issue for the client-centred therapist. No matter how the client presents himself and no matter what his psychiatric diagnosis is, the client-centred therapist will apply his full attention to acceptant, empathic understanding of his client, and to the checking of the accuracy of this understanding with the client. Doing this, he consistently receives the client with unconditional positive regard. In psychiatric contexts, however, this process entails some rather characteristic features and difficulties for the therapist, which are related to the psychiatric diagnosis of the client. It is helpful for the therapist to know about these characteristics and difficulties in order not to lose confidence, neither in his competence as a therapist, nor in the theory of client-centred therapy, nor in the client's process, as these characteristics and difficulties unfold in his relationship with the client. Therefore, I have organised the material of this book according to these three broadly defined, but conspicuous, psychiatric diagnostic categories, and, when useful for my purpose, I have labelled the people I write about with the psychiatric diagnosis allocated to them. This means that, throughout the book, I shall speak interchangeably from the point of view of the person-centred approach and from the point of view of the medical model of psychiatry, as is most useful. I will clarify this duality in the section about the client-centred therapist's relating with the professionals of the psychiatric landscape, (see p. 29).

I hope that no-one will take offence at the liberties I have taken for the sake of easy and useful reading in the ways the inhabitants of this landscape are grouped and described.

The rationale of the book

I have had several intentions in writing this book. One, though, has been more important to me than the others: first and foremost, I hope the book will benefit all the persons in psychiatric contexts by attracting client-centred therapists to the field of psychiatry.

I am of the opinion that psychiatry today is in dire need of a humanistic revitalisation. The last 10–20 years have seen an ascendance of biological explanations of the ailments of patients, and new medicines have been developed to ease their pains. Concomitantly, there has been a demand on psychotherapy to become ever more goal-directed, manualised, cost-benefit effective and adaptable to the medical model. There is nothing inherently wrong with this development, but seen from my vantage point it has taken place at the expense of understanding patients.

Understanding patients is a very different endeavour from explaining their ailments. Understanding and explaining are fundamentally different activities, they belong in different dimensions of research into the human condition, and they are as incomparable as is the length of a stretch of time to the length of a stretch of road. Will an explanation of how 'the taste of chocolate' comes about help you understand the meaning of 'the taste of chocolate', or help you understand how chocolate tastes? In psychiatry, however, there has been a still more dominating tendency to confuse explaining with understanding, whether the explanation is regarded to be biological or psychological. The importance of listening to the patient and understanding how he views himself, others, and the world, has diminished in psychiatry over the last couple of decades, to the detriment of patients, however positively psychiatry may have developed in other directions.

Client-centred theory and the medical model do seem to be quite antithetical. Client-centred theory stresses that the client is the best expert about himself, whereas the medical model stresses that the therapist (doctor, nurse, etc.) is the best expert about the patient. This expert knows, after examination, what is wrong with the patient (diagnosis) and how to remedy this by prescribing the treatment that is right for this specifically diagnosed disease.

With most somatic diseases client-centred theory and the medical model do not come into contact. Most people who regard an ailment of theirs as somatic or physical seek out a doctor to help them, and they expect and want the doctor to be the expert: someone who examines, diagnoses, and prescribes treatment. Indeed, this is what he most often does.

When it comes to psychological problems and ailments the picture is far more complex. There are pharmacological treatments and there are schools of psychotherapy with a medical model foundation where the therapist is the expert, which is fundamentally the case in, for example, psychoanalytic therapy and cognitive-behavioural therapy. There is also, however, client-centred therapy with its conviction of the existence of the actualising tendency and therefore, by implication, a view of the client as the best expert on himself. There is much heated debate among the practitioners of these different treatment approaches, about which of them offers the best help to clients with psychological problems. Each has its own explanations for such problems and each can point to research evidence which legitimises the particular treatment approach of each of them.

Within the medical discipline of psychiatry, these issues are very clearly in the foreground, because patients usually do not receive just one, but several forms of treatment (psychotherapy and medicine and physiotherapy, for example), so staff members have to work together with mutual respect in order to be of greatest possible benefit to the patients. This can be difficult when the staff members' frames of reference seem mutually exclusive; antagonism can easily develop and different camps declare themselves 'at war' with each other, each camp claiming to know the 'truth'. In such an atmosphere, there is great risk of 'burnout' among staff members and of far less than optimal treatment of patients.

The client-centred therapist, in particular, with his conviction that the client is the best expert on himself, can find it difficult to work in a setting where everyone else is regarded as, regards themselves to be, and, within the context of each of their disciplines, actually is, an expert on the patients. They are, from their frames of reference, experts on what is wrong with the patients and on what kinds of treatment are best for the patients. However, if the client-centred therapist and the practitioners of the medical model can work together with respect for each other's viewpoint, the client-centred therapist will find that he has much to offer in this setting and that his work is exciting and stimulating.

It is my contention that understanding (in the theory of client-centred therapy), and explaining (in the medical model theory of psychiatry), are complementary, not contradictory, activities. It is therefore also my contention that client-centred therapists who regard their work as being antithetical, antagonistic and contradictory to the medical model of psychiatry are making the mistake of comparing fundamentally incomparable approaches. In order to be of service to everybody in a given psychiatric context, the client-centred therapist must work with respect for the medical model of psychiatry without compromising the philosophy inherent in his own work. The first section of this book, therefore, deals with ways in which the client-centred therapist can relate positively with the medical model of psychiatry. I am convinced that therapy with psychiatric clients fails just as often because the therapist does not know how to relate with the psychiatric context of the client (i.e. staff members), as it fails because the therapist does not know how to relate with the clients.

This does not mean that the client-centred therapist will not experience conflicts of values when working within a psychiatric context. It is particularly the case for involuntary admittances, involuntary detainments, and involuntary treatments 'for the sake of the patient'. The concept of the freedom of the individual to make his own decisions on his own behalf and the notion of each person being the best expert on himself are central to the philosophy of client-centred therapy and precious to client-centred therapists. To the client-centred therapist, therefore, some of the practices of psychiatry will be experienced as tantamount to violating the rights of the individual. As I see it, it is up to the individual to decide whether working within a system that applies these kinds of interventions is contrary to one's own ethics or not. Psychiatry in all western democracies is obliged by national legislations to force itself on some people. The question, therefore, is not primarily a question of conflict between the philosophy of the person-centred approach and the philosophy of the medical model of psychiatry; it is a question of a broader political/ethical discussion and conflict about which values each of us wants to see advanced in the society of which we are a part. I find a conflict of values with the legislation about the application of force in psychiatry, not with my colleagues in the psychiatric context, whose actions are constrained and determined by this legislation, and who sometimes share these self-same value conflicts with me.

Seeing these issues solely as points of conflict between the philosophy of the person-centred approach and the philosophy of the medical model is, in my opinion, too narrow a viewpoint. Such a viewpoint runs the risk of making it virtually impossible for the client-centred therapist to work in many psychiatric services and also risks turning the patients of psychiatry into 'hostages' in a 'war' of values between the client-centred therapist and the representatives of the medical model. The patients of psychiatry will benefit from neither. This said, it is also true that deep questions about ethics and values make themselves strongly and vividly felt in the context of psychiatry. To me, this has been one of the challenges and attractions of working in a psychiatric context, rather than one of the drawbacks. Some of the major ethical questions that arise in the context of psychiatry will be discussed further as they arise naturally on the following pages.

On the other hand, it is also the case that the client-centred therapist depends on respect from the psychiatric establishment to do his work in this context. In a psychiatric context, the manager(s) of the client-centred therapist will most often be a person trained in the medical model of thinking, typically a psychiatrist. As a basic starting point the client-centred therapist must have his viewpoint — that the client is the best expert on himself — respected as far as his own relationship with his clients is concerned, even though his manager(s) work(s) from a different philosophical orientation. If it is required that the client-centred therapist in any way takes the role of being an expert on his clients, he can, of course, no longer work as a client-centred therapist. I have been fortunate to work in a setting that has respected and valued my client-centred philosophical orientation as a necessary complementation to the more dominant philosophical orientation of the medical model.

A second major intention for me in writing this book has been to counter the myth that client-centred therapy is only useful for clients with 'neurotic' or 'existential' problems, that it is not helpful to the psychotic or near-psychotic patients of psychiatry. I have worked for more than 25 years in a psychiatric hospital, applying variously psychoanalytic, cognitive-behavioural, and client-centred therapy in my psychotherapeutic work with clients, and it has been my experience that client-centred therapy has a far wider applicability than other psychotherapies. Besides being applicable with clients who can also benefit from other psychotherapies, client-centred therapy, in addition, accommodates those clients who are sensitive and resistant to the therapist being the expert on the client. Furthermore, with the extra approach of the very concrete level of empathising of the so-called contact reflections of pre-therapy (Prouty, 1994), the client-centred therapist can also relate acceptantly and empathically with patients who are normally experienced as being 'out of contact' and out of 'therapeutic reach' of other schools of psychotherapy. Finally, many of those persons who regard themselves as prisoners of psychiatry will accept and appreciate an offer of person-centred interaction as a welcome and beneficial refuge from other staff members' active efforts at changing their perceptions of reality.

There exist several research studies on the effect of client-centred therapy with patients diagnosed as suffering from schizophrenia. The scope of this book does not allow an overview of this whole field; instead, interested readers are referred to Garry Prouty's excellent paper, 'Humanistic psychotherapy for people with schizophrenia' (2002). Only the results of a few of the major research studies will be described in the following paragraphs.

In the early 1960s, Carl Rogers headed a comprehensive and carefully designed research project, the 'Wisconsin Project' (Rogers et al., 1967), with the intention of studying the effects of client-centred therapy on patients diagnosed with schizophrenia. The results were not unequivocally positive with respect to the beneficial effect of client-centred therapy with this population, but when one reads the book about the project, there seem to be many reasons, extraneous to client-centred therapy as such, for this result. I'll expand on this in the section about client-centred therapy with psychotic clients (see p. 59).

In 1983, Ludwig Teusch headed a more modest research study on client-centred therapy with schizophrenic clients in Essen Psychiatric University Hospital (Teusch et al., 1983). In 1990 Teusch reports on this study with the following conclusions: 'Client-centred therapy can be regarded as helpful and effective in the treatment of schizophrenic patients. However, client-centred therapy, as other psychotherapeutic approaches, is not the method of choice; it is necessary to integrate it into a multidimensional therapy plan which mainly includes social intervention and neuroleptic drug therapy' (p. 642). Further, Teusch states: 'Standard conditions with regular individual and/or group therapy sessions are only possible or useful if the psychopathological symptomatology is not acute nor severe, and if the patient is at least minimally motivated in psychotherapy. If these conditions are taken into account, nearly all patients benefit from treatment in a measurable way' (p. 642).

Furthermore, there is research evidence for the beneficial effect of pre-therapy with autistic and retarded psychotic patients (Prouty, 1994), a group of people that is not 'minimally motivated in psychotherapy' and whose symptomatology is severe, i.e. persons who would not benefit from the ordinary client-centred therapy of the Essen study.

A third intention of writing this book has been to give an impression of the therapy process with psychiatric clients for the benefit of client-centred therapists. Most psychiatric clients are relatively hard to understand and will typically be considered 'difficult'. Knowing about the characteristics of the therapy processes with these clients will hopefully be of use to client-centred therapists, whether inside or outside the context of psychiatry, when they find their clients 'difficult'. It is supportive to know that difficulties such as impasses, not understanding, feeling 'out of contact', feeling helpless etc., are part of the process and not necessarily a sign of potential therapeutic failure.

A fourth and concluding intention has been to summarise, and clarify to myself, almost 30 years of experience with psychotherapy within the context of psychiatry. Writing this book has been, for me, an experience rich in pleasure, challenge, clarification, and learning, and it has deepened my understanding of, and dedication to, the theory of Carl Rogers, as he laid it out in *Client-Centered Therapy* (1951).

PART ONE
THE AUTHOR'S CONCEPTUALISATION
OF CLIENT-CENTRED THEORY

THE BASIC CONCEPTS

In writing the main sections of this book, I have assumed that the reader has a basic familiarity with the theory of client-centred therapy, particularly as Carl Rogers formulated it in his book, *Client-Centered Therapy* (1951). This may, of course, not be the case, which is one of my reasons for including this brief theoretical introduction. Another reason is that somewhat diverging ways of understanding and defining the key concepts of the theory exist within the community of client-centred therapists, and therefore also diverging ways of applying client-centred therapy. The third reason is to clarify the difference, in my own practice, between client-centred therapy and the broader concept of what I call person-centred interaction. It therefore seems appropriate that, from the outset, I should make it clear how the key concepts of client-centred therapy and person-centred interaction are conceptualised and defined in this book. As the scope of the book does not allow a thorough discussion of these issues, my understanding of the key concepts of the theory will be presented in a relatively short and declarative form.

As the central tenets of the theory of client-centred therapy, Rogers hypothesised the existence of the actualising tendency (1959, p. 196), and he hypothesised the following conditions as being necessary and sufficient for therapeutic change to occur (1959, p. 213, original emphasis):

1. That two persons are in *contact*.
2. That the first person, whom we shall term the client, is in a state of *incongruence*, being *vulnerable*, or *anxious*.
3. That the second person, whom we shall term the therapist, is *congruent* in the *relationship*.
4. That the therapist is *experiencing unconditional positive regard* towards the client.
5. That the therapist is *experiencing* an *empathic* understanding of the client's *internal frame of reference*.
6. That the client *perceives*, at least to a minimal degree, conditions 4 and 5, the *unconditional positive regard* of the therapist for him, and the *empathic* understanding of the therapist.

Divergent ways of understanding the theory among person-centred practitioners emerge predominantly with respect to the following five issues:

1. The more concrete and detailed meanings of the above-mentioned key concepts of the theory, for example what it actually means to experience empathic understanding and unconditional positive regard and, in even greater detail, what it means that the therapist's experience of positive regard for the client is unconditional.
2. The relation, if any, between the fundamental hypothesis in the theory of personality, i.e. the hypothesis of the existence of the actualising tendency on the one hand, and the theory of therapy on the other hand.
3. The interrelationship and relative importance of the three so-called 'core conditions', namely congruence, unconditional positive regard, and empathic understanding.
4. The communicative aspect of client-centred therapy, i.e. the question of how the therapist communicates his experience of empathic understanding of the client, and his experience of unconditional positive regard for the client, in order that the sixth condition can be met, and the question whether this shall be specified, at all, or not.
5. The question whether a non-directive attitude is inherent to client-centred therapy or not.

My own understanding of the essence of Rogers' theory of therapy is as follows:

> *If* the actualising tendency exists, *then* the therapist's consistent presence in the tentative, acceptant, empathic understanding response process is necessary and sufficient to facilitate actualisation of the client's most constructive potentials.

Because I am convinced of the existence of the inherent pro-social or positive disposition of the organism that is implied in the concept of the actualising tendency, by the experiences of my life, in general, and by the experience of client-centred therapy being helpful to my clients, in particular, I do my best, when working as a therapist, to be consistently present in the tentative, acceptant, empathic understanding response process with my client. In addition, I do my best to do neither more nor less than this.

I am indebted to Barbara Brodley (1998, p. 24) for the phrase 'the empathic understanding response process'. My understanding of the concept in the statement above is as follows.

1. The pro-social or positive disposition of the actualising tendency

The organism is actualised along genetically determined lines and according to the positive and negative consequences, as perceived, of its behaviour. Further, the organism is positively and pro-socially directional. This means that the organism is always actualised as constructively and pro-socially as its past and present conditions, or reinforcement contingencies, permit. This does not imply any notion that human beings are inherently 'good' — nor 'bad' for that matter. It implies that human beings are born with a vast repertoire of potentials, some more or less constructive, others more or less destructive. Which of these are actualised will depend on current living conditions, but it will always be the most constructive ones possible under these conditions.

This way of understanding the concept of the actualising tendency has the advantage of avoiding the concept of 'self-actualisation'. I find this concept problematic when it is taken to imply actualisation of one's 'true' self (in contrast to a 'false' self or false concept of self) as a kind of in-born entity which the actualising tendency strives to make blossom or come to fruition. I am doubtful about the notion of 'becoming that which one was meant to become'. The problem is how can anyone know what one was 'meant' to become, and 'meant' by whom? We may think, for example, that gorillas are meant to become more or less like the stereotypical gorillas of the jungle. However, when we look at the gorillas of Francine Patterson (1990), who display a vastly greater communicative repertoire than that of gorillas in their 'natural' environment, it is appropriate to put a question mark against the notion of the 'true' nature of the gorilla, and, by implication, against the notion of the 'true' self of the human being. The experience, as I see it, of behaving according to one's 'true self', or the experience of 'actualising oneself', simply means engaging in those kinds of behaviours which are experienced as rewarding or satisfying. Likewise, the experience of freedom, or choosing freely, is equivalent to doing that which is experienced as having rewarding or satisfying consequences, without fear of punishment.

Therefore, my way of understanding the basic axiom of the client-centred theory of personality, that of the hypothesis of the existence of the actualising tendency, comes much closer to the behaviourist notion, that behaviour is controlled by rewarding consequences, than to the notion of actualising a 'true' self. This may be a somewhat unfamiliar way of thinking about the actualising tendency for many client-centred therapists, but it was not wholly unfamiliar to Rogers. In his dialogue with Skinner (June 11 and 12, 1962, published in Kirschenbaum and Henderson, 1989) he says (p. 132):

> I am in thorough agreement with Dr. Skinner that, viewed from the external, scientific, objective perspective, man is determined by genetic

and cultural influences. I have also said that in an entirely different dimension, such things as freedom and choice are extremely real. I see it as being similar to the situation in physics where you can prove that the wave theory of light is supported by evidence, as is the corpuscular theory, though the two of them appear to be contradictory. They are not, at the present state of knowledge, reconcilable, but one would be narrowing his perception of physics to deny one or the other. It is in this same sense that I regard both of these dimensions as real, although they exist in paradoxical relationship. [Physicists, today, would not talk of a paradoxical relationship, but of a complementary relationship.]

2. Consistent presence

'Consistent presence' is the way I define 'congruence' within a client-centred therapeutic relationship. It means that the therapist is absorbed, from the start of the session to the end of the session, in the tentative, acceptant, empathic understanding response process with the client, that he is 100% present in this process, that he, for the duration of the session, puts aside his own worries, values, opinions, etc. In short: the therapist has put himself 'out of the way of the client', he feels comfortable doing this, and he feels that he is himself, whole and integrated, in his engagement with nothing but the tentative, acceptant, empathic understanding response process with his client. I think most people will recognise what I mean with 'consistent presence' when they think of the experience of being engaged with, and absorbed in, something they love to do, be it reading a book, playing football, gardening, making love, cooking, solving a mathematical problem, or whatever. When engaged like that, there is simply no room for a 'professional front' or 'personal façade', which is another, frequently employed way, of understanding the concept of therapist congruence.

Therefore, the way I define 'congruence' does not mean that the therapist does not express his personality in the relationship with the client. First of all, practising client-centred therapy is, in and of itself, an expression of the therapist's personality: the choice to do client-centred therapy, rather than some other form of therapy, is normally associated with values that are deeply held by the therapist. Second, the therapist expresses his personality in many minor ways: by his non-verbal behaviour and tone of voice, by his language style and style of dressing, by the surroundings in which he receives clients, etc., i.e. by his whole way of being as he engages in the therapeutic process with the client. In short, the therapist has his own unique way of being consistently present in the tentative, acceptant, empathic understanding response process, just as the football player has his own unique way of being absorbed in what he's doing and at the same time doing it according to the 'conceptualisation', or rules, of football.

However, this way of defining 'congruence', also means that I see no place for therapist self-disclosures in the course of therapy, and furthermore it means that the therapist, ordinarily, does not let himself be directed to his own frame of reference by the client, i.e. when the client asks him some question or makes some request of him. This is the point where I discriminate between my client-centred therapy practice and my person-centred practice. When engaged in person-centred practice I do respond from my own frame of reference when requested to by the other person in the interaction, because this interaction is not defined as therapy by the other person. I will expand this issue further in a later section, on the universality of client-centred therapy (see p. 18).

3. Tentative

'Tentative' means that the therapist is never sure that his empathic understanding of the client is accurate, and that his acceptant, empathic understanding responses are regarded, or more or less explicitly formulated, as hypotheses for the client to confirm or refute, whether the client does this verbally, or non-verbally, or not at all. The client is the final judge of the degree to which the therapist's understanding is accurate. Formulating one's responses in a clearly tentative way can be important with many psychiatric clients, whose locus of evaluation is often externalised. They can easily be 'overpowered' into 'confirming' more declaratively formulated responses as the truth about them, because their sense of themselves is relatively fragile and inconsistent.

4. Acceptant

'Acceptant' means that the therapist receives all client expressions with unconditional positive regard. Unconditional positive regard is a hard concept to come to terms with. It has been very helpful for me to ask myself: 'Regard for what?' My personal answer is a consequence of my conviction of the existence of the inherent constructive, pro-social, disposition of the human organism. This means that I feel unconditional positive regard for the client because I am convinced that he is making the most constructive contribution to the human condition that he is capable of with the possibilities available to him in his current phenomenological field. In short, at all times the client is doing the best he can with respect to his current conditions of living.

This evidently implies that the 'unconditional' in unconditional positive regard means that the therapist does not value any client expression higher than any other, that all the client's expressions are received by the therapist with equal acceptance.

It does not mean that the client may not do better, may not make contributions that are more constructive, and may not actualise more self-enhancing potentials. If conditions become more facilitating of actualisation of the more constructive potentials of the client, and especially with the conditions of client-centred therapy, the phenomenological field of the client will change, i.e. he will learn more, and become more wise, about himself, others, and the world, and more constructive possibilities will thereby become available to him. In addition, he, himself, will influence his living conditions in a positive direction by behaving more constructively; i.e. interdependent feedback processes are at play between a person's behaviour and his living conditions, particularly, of course, his social environment.

This also implies that good and evil does not exist as such. To me, 'being good' is having wisdom or being knowledgeable about oneself, others, and the world, and 'being evil' is being ignorant about oneself, others, and the world. The horrendous, cruel, hateful acts done by people, to themselves, others, and the world, are expressions of misunderstandings and ignorance, i.e. they are, in short, mistakes. The fact that mistakes can have the most awfully harmful consequences, including genocide, is another matter.

I do not imply, by this, that limits should not be put on what one considers to be harmful behaviour. Of course, one should seek to prevent and limit such behaviour. What I do suggest, is that such behaviour should not be punished. The wish to punish is, to me, antithetical to a conviction of the existence of the pro-social disposition of human beings and to a genuine feeling of unconditional positive regard towards others and towards oneself.

5. Empathic understanding

I define 'empathic understanding' very simply; namely as understanding that which the client wants the therapist to understand. In the formulation, 'that which the client wants the therapist to understand', two things are implied: (1) that the understanding is from the client's frame of reference, and (2) that the understanding is accurate, meaning that the therapist understands neither more nor less than the client wants him to understand.

I do not systematically aim at the 'edge of awareness' experiences of the client (Mearns and Thorne, 1999, p. 52) or at 'additive empathy' (ibid. p. 45), because I find these to be subtle conveyances of conditional regard for the client's actual choice of experiential level. More will be said about this in the section about near-psychotic clients (p. 118).

6. Response

The therapist's empathic understanding will not be of much use to the client unless it is somehow communicated to the client, verbally and/or non-verbally. This is done in the empathic understanding response process (Brodley, 1996, p. 22 ff). Personally, I liked the earlier term 'empathic reflection', because I see this as the behavioural hallmark of client-centred therapy, and in many ways, I regret the diminished use of this term, although I appreciate and understand why Rogers came to dislike it. I agree with the following statement of John Shlien, quoted as a personal communication in Rogers' (1986) discussion of the issue:

> '*Reflection*' is unfairly damned. It was rightly criticized when you described the wooden mockery it could become in the hand of insensitive people, and you wrote beautifully on that point. But you neglected the other side. It is an instrument of artistic virtuosity in the hands of a sincere, intelligent, empathic listener. It made possible the development of client-centred therapy, when the philosophy alone could not have. Undeserved denigration of the technique leads to fatuous alternatives in the name of 'congruence.'

How the therapist expresses his tentative, acceptant, empathic understanding of the client's expressions of himself, i.e. the way empathic reflections are expressed, is one of the facets of client-centred therapy that is most uniquely dependent on the personality of the therapist. The issue of *when* the therapist expresses his empathic understanding of the client has been discussed eloquently by Barbara Brodley (1998).

7. Process

From start to finish of a session, the therapist is engaged and absorbed in an ever-changing relationship with the client. The therapist's part of this relationship is his process of continually changing, tentative, empathic understanding of the client, and his expressions of this understanding to the client. There is nothing stationary about this: it is a continuous 'holding and letting go' of the therapist's momentary understanding — and particularly with psychotic clients this process can include periods of not understanding anything at all.

8. Constructive potentials

I use this term very loosely and broadly, allowing each person (including clients) to define the term more narrowly and concretely according to his own judgement and values. Rogers (1959, pp. 234–5 and 1961, Chapter 9) did create a picture of the 'fully functioning person', which he regarded as an asymptote[1], i.e. a limit one can get infinitely close to, but never reach (1959, p. 235). One of the characteristics of Rogers' 'fully functioning person' is 'openness to experience', which means that the 'fully functioning person' is continuously in a process of change as he accurately symbolises his experiences in awareness, without denial or distortion (Rogers, 1959, pp. 206 and 234). I am inclined to think of being open to one's experiences, or of becoming increasingly open to one's experiences, as synonymous with, or implying, actualisation of the person's most constructive potentials, as the hallmark of psychological health and positive psychological development. Likewise, I think of denial, and distortion of experiences, as actualising potentials that are more destructive — but it is still actualisation of the most constructive potentials possible with respect to current living conditions.

In the section about near-psychotic clients (see p. 118), several examples will be given which illustrate how therapist errors can facilitate actualisation of the more destructive, rather than more constructive, potentials of the client.

With the above conceptualisation of client-centred therapy, I position myself among those client-centred therapists variously called 'traditional', 'classical', 'purist', 'non-directive', and 'orthodox'. Even within this group of therapists, my understanding of client-centred therapy is probably somewhat 'radical'. This is because my definition of the essence of client-centred therapy is behavioural, i.e. responding with tentative, acceptant, empathic understanding, or acceptant, empathic reflection, is what, to me, delineates client-centred therapy from all other therapies. It is also because I advocate empathising with clients' requests for responses from the therapist's own frame, instead of accommodating these requests.

My rationale for choosing this conceptualisation of client-centred therapy is six-fold:

1. Consistently responding with tentative, acceptant, empathic understanding is, to me, equivalent to maximally minimising the risk of conveying conditional regard to the client.
2. This conceptualisation of client-centred therapy clearly delineates client-centred therapy from what I would call 'eclectic therapies' based on client-centred therapy.
3. Its focus on the behaviour, rather than the experience, of the therapist places it squarely within a scientific framework.

---

1. Asymptote — a mathematical expression for something which gets closer and closer to a value without ever actually getting there.

4. It is faithful to Rogers' own behaviour in therapy, as documented by many audiotapes and videotapes of Rogers' sessions.
5. Trying to fulfil my wish to become the therapist I want to be, i.e. doing my best to work according to the above conceptualisation of client-centred therapy, has been, to me, the single, most decisive, factor in my personal and professional development.
6. With this conceptualisation of client-centred therapy, I love practising therapy.

Many people have been instrumental in my development of the above conceptualisation of client-centred therapy. Besides those already mentioned, I would additionally mention Jerold Bozarth (1998), and Marvin Frankel (personal correspondence, May 2000–May 2002).

ON THE UNIVERSALITY OF CLIENT-CENTRED THERAPY

The above conceptualisation of client-centred therapy is not assumed to be universal, i.e. I do not assume that it holds true for all persons.

From my experience with the patients of psychiatry, these persons seem to me to organise themselves naturally into three groups (with overlaps, of course), which I'll describe briefly.

1. Most patients in psychiatric contexts belong to the ordinary client population of client-centred therapy. By this I mean that the patient is voluntary and self-expressive, i.e. if he sees a therapist, he initiates freely and voluntarily, contact with the therapist, and he wants the therapist to understand something about himself and his life. It was in work with these clients that Rogers and his co-workers developed the theory and practice of client-centred therapy at the Chicago Counseling Center in the 1950s. Likewise, it is for patients belonging to this group that I assume that the above conceptualisation of client-centred therapy holds true. Almost all adult persons, outside of prisons, psychiatric hospitals, and psychiatric nursing homes, belong to this client population, if they seek the help of a psychotherapist.

2. Some patients do not seem to be self-expressive, and for this reason alone it is impossible to know the degree to which the patient considers himself to be voluntarily in contact with the client-centred therapist. They are ordinarily experienced as being more or less 'out of contact'. They are termed 'autistic' and 'withdrawn' in the psychiatric vocabulary. With these persons, it will ordinarily be the client-centred therapist who initiates the contact, and, at the outset, at least, they do not seem to want him to understand anything about them. With these 'pre-expressive' persons, of course, client-centred therapy, as conceptualised above, is an impossibility, first because one does not know whether they see themselves as voluntarily participating in the relationship or not, and second because 'empathic understanding', in this conceptualisation, is defined as an understanding of the client's inner frame of reference. The client-centred therapist, however, rarely experiences an 'inner' frame of reference with these persons since there is, seemingly, nothing about their inner goings on they want to disclose to the therapist. Garry Prouty (1994) has developed 'pre-therapy' as a person-centred way of relating with 'pre-expressive' persons and coined the evocative term 'pre-expressive' to designate an essential quality of the contact with these persons. The so-called 'contact reflections' of pre-therapy, which allow the client-centred therapist to empathise on a sufficiently concrete level to relate acceptantly with pre-expressive persons, will be one of the subjects of the section

about therapy with so-called psychotic persons (see p. 70).

3. Many 'patients', particularly in the closed wards of psychiatric hospitals, are self-expressive, but certainly not voluntary. The only thing they want is to be released. They are, most often, seen as floridly paranoid, megalomaniac, manic, and sometimes as psychotically depressed, by the medical model representatives of psychiatry. They are the prisoners of psychiatry. If the client-centred therapist has contact with these persons, it is on his own initiative, out of his own interest, and the prisoner may, at least in the beginning, allow this contact as a nice way of passing the time of detainment. The prisoners will typically resist any definition of the relationship as being 'therapeutic', since they do not regard themselves as mentally ill, and therefore do not wish any kind of treatment, whether medical or psychotherapeutic. A person-centred relationship with these persons, though, can sometimes develop into an ordinary therapy relationship, where the former prisoner, now client, does want to meet with the client-centred therapist as therapist, i.e. he now wants the relationship to be a therapeutic relationship in the ordinary sense of this word. Furthermore, many patients, albeit not formally involuntary, are somewhat non-responsive to an offer of psychotherapy, and it is the client-centred therapist's wish to get to know and understand them that 'energises' the contact. Finally, although they come by themselves to see the therapist, some patients come reluctantly or hesitantly, as a result of persuasion by others.

As long as it is the client-centred therapist who initiates the contact, or as long as the client-centred therapist is convinced that the person, with whom he relates, feels that the choice to be in the relationship is not fully his own, it is important not to conceptualise the relationship as an ordinary client-centred therapeutic relationship.

I stated above that it is inherent in my conceptualisation of client-centred therapy that the therapist remains in the tentative, acceptant, empathic understanding response process *also* when the client, verbally or non-verbally, directs the therapist to his, the therapist's, own frame of reference, by asking some question or making some request of the therapist. This means that I do not answer questions, but continue to try to understand the client empathically, when the client asks a question of me. This, of course, is not synonymous with ignoring the question; on the contrary, it means that my empathic understanding includes empathic understanding of the questioning/requesting client. As already mentioned, I find this to be the safest way to avoid conveying conditional regard to clients with whom I have an ordinary client-centred therapeutic relationship. I am, of course, not including questions about the practical arrangements for the therapy (place, time, etc.), and neither am I including questions which the client might ask of any person in the vicinity, like, 'When is the next bus leaving?' or, 'Can I have a glass of water?' Such questions I'd classify as 'emergency questions'. What I do include are all kinds of requests for advice from the therapist, or questions about the therapist's private affairs, or personal opinions of this and that, since I most often experience such requests as more or less subtle requests for the therapist's conditional regard.

In this respect, I am probably at variance with most client-centred practitioners (see, for example, Brodley, 1999).

However, with patients who do not actively define their relationship with me as a therapeutic relationship, i.e. with pre-expressive persons and with prisoners, who are actually doing me a favour by allowing me to have contact with them, I let myself be directed to my own frame of reference. This is, of course, also the case with my interaction with other staff members. I normally respond from my own frame of reference, when requested to do so, and to the degree my personal limits permit, in order to respect that the other person does not define himself as a client in his or her relationship with me. It is in these cases I regard myself as a 'person-centred practitioner' rather than a client-centred therapist. Therefore, the question of accommodating, or not, the other person's requests for responses from my own frame is what makes the difference between my person-centred interaction practice and my client-centred therapy practice. I find the first appropriate with people who are 'pre-expressive', with the prisoners of psychiatry, and in many of my interactions with other staff members. I find the second appropriate with those who actively define themselves as clients and have a therapeutic relationship as their highest priority in our interaction. This way of distinguishing between 'person-centred practice', and 'client-centred therapy' is, I know, very unusual. It has been necessitated by my wish to make sense of the way I try to be of the greatest possible use to all the inhabitants of the psychiatric landscape, including myself, during my daily hours of work in that landscape.

Client-centred therapy, proper, can only come about with fully self-expressive and fully voluntary clients. This does not mean, however, that the client-centred therapist should not use his competence to offer the most constructive and mutually rewarding relationship of which he is capable, to other inhabitants of the psychiatric landscape.

One of the challenges in person-centred interaction/client-centred therapy with patients (and prisoners) in psychiatric contexts is following and being in tune with them in transitional processes between being pre-expressive and self-expressive, between seeing themselves as prisoners and as clients. Many of the examples in the book will show the empathic understanding responses of ordinary client-centred therapy interspersed with the contact reflections of pre-therapy. Alternatively, they will sometimes show the client-centred therapist letting himself be directed to his own frame of reference by a pre-expressive person or a psychiatric prisoner who has allowed the therapist to be in contact with them.

The universality of client-centred therapy takes on a different dimension when seen from the perspective of the goals of therapy. Patterson (1995) has written about the ultimate, mediate and immediate goals of the psychotherapist (not only client-centred therapists, but therapists from all schools of psychotherapy). In my understanding of Patterson's terms, the ultimate goal of the psychotherapist is the positive growth and development of the client, whatever this may be, and in the broadest sense of these terms. According to their respective theories, the psychoanalyst, for example, wants to see his client heading securely towards 'where the id was, shall the ego be', and the client-centred therapist wants to see him heading towards 'fully functioning'. What this means in more detail, and for any given client, though, can first be known at termination of the therapy. The therapist has no idea, from the start, what the client will be like at termination.

The mediate goal of the psychotherapist is that the client learns how to solve his presenting problem(s). This normally comes about as a 'by product' in therapies which primarily work towards ultimate goals, like client-centred therapy and psychoanalysis proper, whereas other therapies, like cognitive-behavioural therapy and short-term psychoanalytic therapy, work in a more goal-directed and focused way towards mediate goals. The therapist's aim in these therapies is more narrowly to teach the client the necessary skills or give him the necessary insight to solve his presenting problems, and therapy terminates when this goal has been reached. The therapist has, from the start, a quite specific idea of what the client will be like at termination. In this case, it is the positive growth and development of the client, in the broad sense, which may be the 'by product' of the therapy. This will be the case when the mediate goal is in accordance with the client's openness to his own experience, i.e. the goal is not the result of some internalised conditions of worth, or fear of punishment, in the broadest sense of the term 'punishment'.

One could say that the therapist who works towards ultimate goals has the person as the focus of his attention — he is 'person-oriented' — whereas the therapist who works towards mediate goals has the problem as the focus of his attention — he is 'problem-oriented' (see also Bozarth, 1998, p. 24).

Finally, the immediate goal of the therapist is to work as skilfully and competently as possible, in accordance with his chosen 'school' of psychotherapy, towards either of the two goals mentioned above.

If one imagines a continuum of therapies, from the most 'person-oriented', and those working towards ultimate goals, in one end, and the most 'problem-oriented', and those working towards mediate goals in the other end, I think there can be no doubt that client-centred therapy occupies the most extreme point of the 'person-oriented' and 'growth-oriented' end of this continuum. This means, in my experience, that the therapist's possibility of applying client-centred therapy has certain limits in actual practice, despite its theoretical universality with all persons who define themselves as clients.

Some of the clients I meet do want psychotherapy, but they also very clearly want their therapist to be 'problem-oriented' rather than 'person-oriented': they want their therapist to direct the process towards a clearly stated mediate goal of theirs. They want to learn how to overcome, circumvent, or solve their problems, which they describe in a carefully delineated way in the first two or three sessions, and they look to the therapist as one who will teach them, much more than they look to the therapist as one who will understand them. In effect, they have the same attitude to their therapist as they have to their GP. With these clients, I sometimes become convinced, within the first few sessions, that I will be better able to be of use to them by applying a more directive, problem-oriented psychotherapeutic approach. I then shift to application of, predominantly, cognitive-behavioural therapy and a relationship which is probably best described as student (or client)-centred teaching. This is the case with around 5% of my clients. (Another option would have been to refer them to a colleague applying a more problem-oriented approach.)

I shall not delve further into the details of this variability in my psychotherapeutic practice. I do find it important, though, to mention it, in a book that has as one of its aims to be of help to client-centred therapists who may consider the possibility of employment within a psychiatric context, or are already employed there. Client-centred therapy, with its stress on the *unconditionality* of unconditional positive regard, demands much of its practitioner, probably more than any other form of therapy. In spite of the theoretical universality of client-centred therapy, therefore, the therapist will sometimes choose wisely if he shifts to a more directive approach with clients who clearly want him to do so, instead of over-taxing his competence as a client-centred therapist. This, I think, is preferable to the use of a directive intervention now and then, when it is deemed helpful by the therapist, which is advocated by some therapists of the person-centred orientation (see for example Cain, 1989 and Kahn, 1999). What does 'now and then' mean? With such a practice, the therapist easily runs the risk of actually beginning to apply some form of eclectic therapy, sliding, more or less without their knowing it, away from the client-centred approach.

Directive interventions may be immediately helpful for the client but, in my opinion, they do not belong in client-centred therapy, because they more or less subtly place the therapist in the role of an expert on the client, i.e. the therapist predicts, expertly, what will, be helpful for the client (see also Sommerbeck, 2003). In addition, by sometimes applying a directive intervention, the therapist risks confusing both himself and the client as to the goal of the therapy: are they working towards the ultimate goal of client-centred therapy or are they working towards the mediate goals of a more directive, problem-oriented approach? In my opinion, the wiser choice is to differentiate clearly between non-directive client-centred therapy, and other, more or less directive, therapeutic approaches.

ON THE RELATIVE IMPORTANCE OF THE THREE CORE CONDITIONS WITH PSYCHIATRIC CLIENTS

In *Empathic: An unappreciated way of being* (1975), Rogers writes:

> I would like briefly to state my views as to the significance of what I see as the three attitudinal elements making for growth, in their relationship to one another.
>
> In the ordinary interactions of life — between marital and sex partners, between teacher and student, employer and employee, or between colleagues — it is probable that congruence is the most important element. Such genuineness involves letting the other person know 'where you are' emotionally. It may involve confrontation, and the personally owned and straightforward expression of both negative and positive feelings. Thus, congruence is a basis for living together in a climate of realness.
>
> But in certain other special situations, caring or prizing may turn out to be the most significant. Such situations include non-verbal relationships — parent and infant, therapist and mute psychotic, physician and very ill patient. Caring is an attitude which is known to foster creativity — a nurturing climate in which delicate, tentative new thoughts and productive processes can emerge.
>
> Then, in my experience, there are other situations in which the empathic way of being has the highest priority. When the other person is hurting, confused, troubled, anxious, alienated, terrified; or when he or she is doubtful of self-worth, uncertain as to identity, then understanding is called for. The gentle and sensitive companionship of an empathic stance — accompanied, of course, by the other two attitudes — provides illumination and healing. In such situations deep understanding is, I believe, the most precious gift one can give to another. (p. 9)

Rogers thereby clearly indicated that he found the relative importance of the three core conditions to be different in different contexts, and in different kinds of relationships.

At the same time, the reader may remember (p. 9) that Rogers, in the sixth condition of therapy, states: 'The client perceives, at least to a minimal degree, the unconditional positive regard of the therapist for him, and the empathic understanding of the therapist.' This seems, to me, to imply that Rogers saw both empathic understanding and unconditional positive regard as equally important therapeutic agents in the ordinary client-centred therapeutic relationship.

Many practitioners of client-centred therapy, though, tend to see unconditional positive regard as the primary therapeutic agent in client-centred therapy. Jerold Bozarth (1998, pp. 83–4), for example, writes that: 'conditionality is the bedrock of Rogers' theory of pathology', and 'Rogers' theoretical foundations for psychological dysfunctions can result in no other conclusion: unconditional positive regard is the curative factor of the theory'. In addition:

> The individual's return to unconditional positive self regard is the crux of psychological growth in the theory ... Rogers hypothesises that one must perceive reception of unconditional positive regard in order to correct the pathological state.

Bozarth (ibid.) also argues from Rogers' theoretical statement (1959) on the parent-child relationship:

> It is the parent's experience of unconditional positive regard towards the child that creates (1) fewer conditions of worth, (2) greater experiencing of the organismic valuing process, and (3) psychological adjustment in the child. Moreover, the parent must have unconditional self-regard to be congruent in the relationship and, hence, to be able to experience unconditional positive regard and empathic understanding of the child's frame of reference. This statement succinctly describes the condition of unconditional positive regard as the curative attitude not only for the client but also the importance of unconditional positive self-regard for the therapist to be congruent. (p. 88)

The sensibility of seeing unconditional positive regard as the primary therapeutic agent is highlighted in work with the clients of psychiatry. Generally, their level of experiencing is more shallow, and their focus of evaluation is more external, than is the case with the ordinary client population of client-centred therapy. They seem less able to be aware of themselves as the agent of their own experiences, and they seem less inclined towards self-reflection. The extreme case is someone diagnosed with schizophrenic hallucinations. The apparently pre-expressive person, too, with whom the client-centred therapist does not experience any inner frame of reference, is also a case in point. With pre-expressive persons, it becomes very evident that it is unconditional positive regard that is the primary therapeutic agent. Logically, of course, it must also be so: if the client-centred therapist has no experience of the inner frame of reference of the other person, how can he offer the kind of empathic understanding that is present in his practice of ordinary client-centred therapy?

It is my contention, therefore, that the importance of empathic understanding of the client's inner frame of reference as an independent therapeutic agent is directly proportional to the degree of self-expressiveness of the client. In my experience, the more self-expressive the client, the more empathic understanding tends to stimulate beneficial self-exploratory behaviour and the attainment of insight. This, though, I tend to see as a fortunate 'side-effect' of empathic understanding, as an extra 'bonus', especially with the more self-expressive clients. The primary role of empathic understanding is still, I think, that of a vehicle or channel for the therapist's experience and expression of unconditional positive regard towards the client, or, alternatively stated, it is the safest way maximally to minimise the risk of conveying conditional regard towards the client. I agree with Bozarth (1998) that basically it is the client's increased self-acceptance, facilitated by the therapist's unconditional positive regard, which primarily makes therapy therapeutic: it is not the attainment of insight. Insight, though, does seem to follow closely in the wake of self-acceptance.

It is, of course, artificial to separate the core conditions of unconditional positive regard, empathic understanding, and congruence, as was done in the first section of this theoretical introduction. The intention with this artificial separation was solely to clarify the way I conceptualise each of the core conditions. Both in theory and in practice, each of the conditions is dependent on the two other conditions; the conditions are interrelated and interdependent. Barbara Brodley has put this beautifully (personal communication, December, 2000):

> The theory tells us that unconditional positive regard is the curative agent — but occurring in the context of the totality of the three conditions plus the inherent nondirective attitude that is implicit.

Brodley then continues to conceptualise the interrelationship of the core conditions in terms of Aristotle's categorisation of causes, i.e. in terms of the formal cause, the material cause, the efficient cause, and the final cause. This categorisation is normally illustrated with the building of a house. The design, say, of an architect is the formal cause, the bricks, mortar, glass, windowpanes, etc., which is used to build the house, is the material cause, the craftsmen's act of actually building the house is the efficient cause, and, finally, somebody's wish for this house is the final cause. With respect to the core conditions, Brodley says that one might see congruence as the formal cause, empathic understanding as the material cause, unconditional positive regard as the efficient cause, and the cure as the final cause. To me, this is a very evocative way of illuminating the interrelationship of the core conditions.

ON THE ROLE OF DEVELOPMENTAL THEORIES

It can be helpful for the therapist to know about various theories of how the symptoms and problems of psychiatric clients come about. Being knowledgeable about this can enhance the therapist's understanding and unconditional positive regard for his client and thereby promote the therapeutic relationship. On the other hand, it can have the opposite consequence, if the therapist, on the basis of a specific developmental theory, is on the lookout for particular traumas, developmental issues, etc., to work through with the client. This can make the therapist's work subtly directive.

Rogers saw psychopathology as coming about by the client having been exposed to various, more or less extreme, conditions of worth or conditional regard (1959, pp. 224–30). Later years have seen diagnostically differentiated variations of this theme within the circle of practitioners of the person-centred approach (see, for example, Lambers, 1994 and Warner, 1991). Knowledge about how human psychological development can become thwarted in different ways can, however, come from many different sources. I have found the theories of psychoanalytic writers like Margaret Mahler *et al.* (1975), Daniel Stern (1985), and D. W. Winnicot (1987) to be helpful in this respect. I have, however, also found the literature of great writers of 'fiction' such as Shakespeare, Dostoyevsky, and a host of others, to be helpful. Biographies of 'difficult to understand' historical personalities, like Ian Kershaw's (2000) Hitler biography, for example, can be helpful, too. All of the writers I have mentioned are concerned with the development of human beings and the human condition under various more or less aversive or growth-promoting circumstances. They may focus on the development of different kinds of 'psychopathology', on the development of different political, religious, or sexual attitudes, on the development of criminality, on the development of addictive, aggressive, or abusive behaviour, or on the development of the optimally functioning, psychologically healthy person. Whatever their focus, they may all be of interest and help to the client-centred therapist by increasing his knowledge of the infinitely varied ways of human development and of being human.

In addition, there is the whole issue of the role played by biological factors in human psychological development.

I find it important, therefore, that the client-centred therapist does not focus on any particular diagnostic developmental theory. Instead, I think the therapist should store all his knowledge and experience of the development of all the unique ways of being human, from whatever source it comes, 'in his bones', to assist him receive his client with unconditional positive regard — and first and foremost learn about his client's particular 'developmental theory' from the client himself.

This book, therefore, will not contain theories of how the specific syndromes of psychiatry may have developed. Interested readers are referred, for example, to the writers mentioned above — and to the clients of psychiatry.

... AND FINALLY A NOTE ON IDEALS AND REALITY

Any theory is, and will be, an ideal abstraction of reality, albeit an abstraction that is, hopefully, reasonably compatible with reality. This means that the client-centred therapist depicted in the above paragraphs is my ideal or 'fully functioning' therapist, the one I want to approach as closely as possible. It also means that the compatibility between this ideal of mine and my actual practice is not always as close as I wish. When I deviate from a relatively close approximation to my ideal, though, I see this as a mistake, i.e. as a signal that there is something I need to learn, that I have some personal development to do, that it is time for self-reflection, consultation, supervision, whatever ... or that it is time for a vacation!

PART TWO
RELATING WITH THE PROFESSIONALS OF PSYCHIATRY

THE COMPLEMENTARITY OF CLIENT-CENTRED THERAPY AND THE MEDICAL MODEL

The seeming mutual exclusivity of the viewpoints of the theories of client-centred therapy and the medical model makes itself strongly felt in psychiatric settings, especially in the two following ways:

1. Client-centred therapy is based on an heuristic/phenomenological model, whereas psychiatry is based on the classic scientific model, i.e. the client-centred therapist strives to understand from the client's frame of reference, whereas the psychiatrist strives to explain from his own (theoretical) frame of reference and treats the client from this point of view. Psychiatry has many explanations — more or less well documented by research — for the diverse conditions of patients: hereditary, biochemical, early environmental, etc. These are seen as causal, aetiological factors, contributing alone or in combination to what is normally considered as discrete, specific disease entities. The client-centred therapist, on the other hand, is in no way concerned with explaining the condition and symptoms of the client. He is solely concerned with trying to understand the client from the client's frame of reference and checking the accuracy of this understanding with the client, thereby communicating his unconditional positive regard for the client. This, according to client-centred theory, is helpful to clients whether there exists an (objective) explanation for their ailment or not. Understanding people and explaining people are, as already mentioned, two very different things.

This corresponds to the German philosopher Dilthey's (1894) distinction between the natural sciences as sciences that explain, and the humanities as sciences that understand.

2. The question of whether a client is psychotic or not (one of the most crucial differential diagnostic questions in psychiatry) is made from the point of view of 'consensual reality', i.e. that which the

majority in a given culture regards as reality. From this point of view, delusions and hallucinations (often prominent symptoms in psychosis), are not real, but from the point of view of the delusional or hallucinating client they are real, and therefore they are real, too, for the client-centred therapist when he is trying empathically to follow and understand the client. The client-centred therapist has to suspend his own sense of reality when in therapy sessions with these clients. (An exception to this occurs sometimes when pre-expressive and/or involuntarily committed persons want to know about the therapist's sense of reality.) Fundamentally, this is in no way different from working with clients who are not psychotic, because the therapist will always strive to understand the client from the client's frame of reference no matter how unfamiliar it may be to the therapist. However, the phenomenological field of psychotic clients is private and different from that of the therapist, and from that of 'consensual reality', to a radical and extreme degree. In the psychiatric setting, therefore, the client-centred therapist feels more acutely that he is shuffling back and forth between his client's sense of reality, when in session, and his own sense of reality, which he probably shares to quite a large extent with most of his colleagues (consensual reality), when the session is finished.

It is necessary for the client-centred therapist in the medical model setting of a psychiatric hospital to find a way to encompass and reconcile within himself these seemingly conflicting viewpoints of understanding or explaining and psychotic reality or consensual reality. It is when he cannot do this that he will tend to see the theories of client-centred therapy and the medical model as opposing each other, as two camps at war with each other. With such a point of view, he will most likely find himself in the midst of the already mentioned frequent and fruitless 'who is right?' discussions with his 'medical model' colleagues. Furthermore, because he is typically in a minority position and not in a management or administrative position he will become more and more alienated and isolated in the setting within which he is working. This is the typical context for the development of 'burnout'.

To avoid this I have found the concept of complementarity exceedingly helpful in my work as a client-centred therapist in a psychiatric hospital and I will therefore explain it rather extensively as follows.

In physics, the concept or principle of complementarity is the standard way of thinking about some strange phenomena in the microcosm of elementary particles[1]. I will illustrate this, using the electron as an

---

[1.] There exist numerous introductory texts, for the layperson, to the 'strange ...

example. An electron cannot be studied directly; physicists use different kinds of experimental set-ups to study the nature of the electron. When they do, the following strange phenomenon materialises: in one kind of experimental set-up, the electron is seen to behave as a particle and in another kind of experimental set-up, the electron is seen to behave as a wave. Logically, particle and wave are mutually exclusive categories: something cannot be both a particle and a wave since the first is discrete (it has precise location and delineation) and the second is continuous (it does not have precise location and delineation). When physicists discovered this state of affairs in the 1920s and 1930s they were not happy about it. They therefore tried to find a 'hidden variable' (something in the electron yet to be discovered), that might sometimes appear as a particle, sometimes as a wave. As they were absolutely unsuccessful in this — the electron really *is* an elementary particle, it cannot be subdivided, and no hidden variable exists — the Danish physicist Niels Bohr introduced the concept of complementarity to make some 'sense' of this wave/particle duality, as it is commonly called. Bohr took the position that in choosing his experimental set-up the physicist chooses whether the electron will be a particle or a wave. Alternatively: depending on the way he chooses to look at the electron, the physicist will decide upon the nature of the electron — wave or particle? However, he cannot, of course, see both at the same time. Bohr said that it is meaningless to ask what the electron 'really' is: you have to look at it to know, and then the nature of it depends on how you look at it, i.e. from your own viewpoint or frame of reference. When not being observed, the electron is said to be in a state of superposition of particle and wave.

The earlier mentioned dualities (understanding/explaining, private reality/consensual reality), can very helpfully be conceptualised as complementary viewpoints in analogy with the wave/particle duality: you see and do different things from the two viewpoints, and what you see and do from one viewpoint is neither more nor less true than what you see and do from the other. However, you cannot hold both viewpoints at the same time; instead, you use one or the other viewpoint depending on your purpose. In therapy sessions, the viewpoint of the client-centred therapist is, of course, that of understanding the private reality of the client. In discussions with colleagues, it may be that of explanation and consensual reality. In addition, the two viewpoints could be said to be in a state of superposition when the therapist does not choose one or the other, i.e. when he is neither trying to understand the private reality of a given client in therapy nor sharing thoughts that might explain the psychotic symptoms of the self-same client in staff meetings.

... phenomena' of elementary particle physics and the principle of complementarity. A couple of my own favourites are Polkinghorne (1984) and Lindley (1996).

Over the years, in the hospital where I work, I have explained the principle of complementarity and its foundation in physics, and it has been my experience that it has been very helpful in contributing to mutual respect between the practitioner of client-centred therapy and the practitioner of the medical/psychiatric model. Being able to employ the principle of complementarity to synthesise their seemingly antithetical viewpoints is felt as a relief to the majority of professionals working in this setting, because the nagging question of who is right, whose viewpoint is the most truthful or real, is resolved, or maybe circumvented, in a meaningful way. In this perspective, the employment of the principle of complementarity can also be seen as an example of the person-centred approach in action: I also try to understand the viewpoints of my medical model colleagues from their frame of reference.

In addition, the knowledge that this principle is employed in physics, which is often taken as a model for other scientific disciplines, makes it even more welcome: when physicists can think like this about their 'simple' objects of study, then it seems even more relevant to do so when the object of study is as complex as the human psyche.

It must be remembered, however, that applying the principle of complementarity, in the way I have described above, is exclusively a result of seeing an analogy between some phenomena of the world of quantum mechanics and some phenomena of the world of psychiatry. I postulate no true identity between these two classes of phenomena. Future research may point to ways of thinking about the many puzzling and seemingly antithetical phenomena of psychiatry that are more fruitful than thinking about them in terms of complementarity.

CLIENT-CENTRED THEORY AND THE QUESTION OF
PSYCHIATRIC DIAGNOSIS

As already stated, psychiatric diagnosis is of no issue in client-centred theory and therapy. The conditions necessary and sufficient for facilitation of the client's most constructive potentials are trusted to be the same for everybody, irrespective of diagnosis. Or seen from another angle: the act of (psychiatric) diagnosing would imply that the therapist is in the position of the expert, he would view the client from his (the therapist's) own frame of reference, the locus of evaluation would be in the therapist, and it would be the therapist, not the client, who knew what was wrong with the client. All this has nothing to do with client-centred therapy; it belongs to the medical model, not to the client-centred model.

This does not mean, however, that the client-centred therapist working in a medical model setting can allow himself to be ignorant about the diagnoses employed in the setting or to regard the work of diagnosing patients, done by other professionals in the setting, as superfluous. In the medical model setting of a psychiatric hospital, for example, it is necessary for the client-centred therapist to acknowledge the necessity of psychiatric diagnostics for other professionals and to know about the main psychiatric diagnoses. There are several reasons for this:

1. Patients from the population of a psychiatric hospital, or other psychiatric contexts, will often ask the therapist questions about their diagnosis and want to discuss all kinds of concerns with regard to this. It is important that the therapist is able to accommodate such a request for information in a qualified way when he deems it appropriate. This, of course, does not mean that the therapist identifies with the medical model, only that he can answer and discuss questions about this model when requested to by the patient and that he does so while still, as far as possible, leaving the locus of evaluation and initiative with the patient by returning to empathise with him or her. (See Barbara Brodley (1999) for an eloquent paper on the combination of empathic understanding with responding from the therapist's own frame of reference.)

2. In a psychiatric hospital, the dominant 'language' is the language of the medical model, including the language of psychiatric diagnosis, and the client-centred therapist must be able to communicate in this language with other staff and professionals when working in this culture. The language of the client-centred therapist is the 'foreign' language in this setting and the client-centred therapist is the 'foreigner'. Although the culture of the client-centred therapist may seem antithetical to the culture of the

psychiatric hospital it is important to learn to respect this culture as you do when working in a culture different from your own. This is also in accordance with the principles of the person-centred approach, and clients, furthermore, do not benefit from their therapist feeling alienated from, or antagonistic towards, the setting that most of these clients feel deeply dependent on for a shorter or longer period of time. Again, this does not mean that the client-centred therapist 'changes identity', and it does not mean that the client-centred therapist cannot contribute positively to the setting, as a whole, from his own person-centred frame of reference. It does mean, though, that in general the therapist must be able to see things from the point of view of the medical model as well as from the point of view of the client-centred model. The principle of complementarity is a great help to the therapist in this regard; it helps him become a respectful and respected 'foreigner' in the culture of psychiatry.

3. Clients come into a psychiatric hospital because they need intensive care and help from different treatment modalities. The client-centred therapist will quickly experience the necessity of psychiatric diagnostics for many treatment modalities, especially for the psychopharmacological treatments that help many clients, in combination with psychotherapy, or without psychotherapy. Furthermore, some clients will not accept an offer of psychotherapy, and some clients' wishes are not best met with psychotherapy.

4. The question of psychiatric diagnosis is central (by law) in decisions concerning involuntary commitment and treatment. These questions are continually discussed — and with good reason — in the psychiatric hospital, and much of this discussion hinges on the diagnostic question: is the patient psychotic or not?

THE PATIENTS FROM THE PSYCHIATRIST'S VIEWPOINT

When meeting a patient for the first time the psychiatrist will typically conduct the interview in a way that makes it possible for him to make a (psychiatric) diagnosis. He has hundreds of diagnoses to choose from, but in reality, he will only try to place the patient within a few, very broad diagnostic categories, because that is all he needs to make decisions about which pharmacological treatment to offer his patient, if any at all.

He will try to find answers to the following questions:

1. Is the patient psychotic? Sometimes this is blatantly evident and sometimes the psychiatrist needs to look for more subtle signs of disturbed sense of consensual reality and disturbed capacity to think along conventional logical lines. If he finds that the patient is psychotic, he will probably offer the client treatment with a neuroleptic (anti-psychotic medicine).
2. Is the patient depressive? Sometimes this is blatantly evident, too, and sometimes the psychiatrist needs to look for more subtle signs of self-incrimination, despair, hopelessness, and diminished energy. If he finds the patient depressive, he will probably offer the patient treatment with anti-depressive medicine. (ECT (electric convulsive treatment) is normally not the first treatment of choice and is, in general, only used when treatment with several kinds of anti-depressive medicine has been tried and has failed, or if a patient's heart condition makes treatment with anti-depressive medicine too risky.)
3. Is it a question of personality disorder? The psychiatrist will be inclined to make this diagnosis if he finds no signs of psychosis or depression. Depending on the complaints of the patient, he might offer the patient treatment with anxiolytic medicine (a sedative), or psychotherapy, or both.

Sometimes the psychiatrist will suggest psychotherapy if he diagnoses a psychotic or depressive condition, too, but rarely as the first treatment of choice. Often it is the psychotherapist who suggests psychotherapy, in conjunction with medicine, for these conditions.

It is the rule rather than the exception that several runs of treatment with first one, then the other, medicine must be tried, or combinations of several medicines must be tried, before the psychopharmacological treatment is deemed reasonably effective. It is symptomatic treatment: it doesn't result in a final 'cure', and sometimes the medicine has very unwanted side-effects that can make both the patient and the psychiatrist wonder whether the condition that is being treated is not to be preferred to the side-effects of the treatment. Finally, some conditions seem resistant to whatever kind of medication is tried; this is most frequent in conditions where autism (the patient does not seem to be in psychological contact) is conspicuous.

No mention has been made here of schizophrenia. Most patients suffering from schizophrenia receive treatment with one neuroleptic or another, but this is not a consequence of the diagnosis of schizophrenia, it is a consequence of the psychotic phenomena, such as delusions and hallucinations, that are characteristic of most schizophrenic conditions, but not all. Furthermore, many conditions exist with these symptoms that are not diagnosed as schizophrenia. These are, ordinarily, also treated with neuroleptic medicine. Sometimes it is very hard for the psychiatrist to make a diagnosis. The way the patient presents himself may fit just as well in one diagnostic category as in another, or it may seem to be a mixture of several diagnostic categories. This has to do with the fact that psychiatric diagnostics are purely symptomatic, not aetiological, i.e. they say nothing about the cause(s) of the condition, in the way that, for example, the diagnosis of diabetes does. This also raises a question that plagues psychiatry: are the different conditions, diagnosed in psychiatry, expressions of discrete disease entities, or are they conditions on a continuum, where one condition changes imperceptibly into the other, from 'normality' at one point to 'schizophrenia' at another?

Nobody has the final answer to this question. The continuum 'solution', though, is by far the best match for my own experience with psychiatric patients.

Nobody has the final answer, either, as to the cause(s) of the conditions seen in psychiatry. The standard explanatory model within psychiatry today (especially for psychosis and depression) is the stress/diathesis model. This model hypothesises that there exists in the individual a more or less pronounced disposition (hereditary and biological) to react with psychosis, or depression, when under (psychological) stress; i.e. when the conditions of the milieu of the person are too frustrating or burdensome for the person to cope with. In this way, psychiatry, today, tries to circumvent the 'nature/nurture' conflict by saying that it is a question of both; sometimes 'nature' is more pronounced than 'nurture', sometimes it is the other way around. The most recent development in psychiatric thinking is an acknowledgement of the fact that mental phenomena can influence biological phenomena just as well as biological phenomena can influence mental phenomena. This, of course, is old news to the layperson: just think of how you may blush when suddenly feeling ashamed and how you may sweat when suddenly feeling anxious, etc. It is imagined in some psychiatric circles today that you will, in the not too distant future, be able to see the effect of psychotherapy, for example, as visual changes in scanning images of the brains of clients.

These ways of thinking should, in my opinion, be warmly welcomed as they help lessen the age-old nature/nurture conflict and the corresponding, but not-quite-as-old, traditional antagonism between the psychiatrist and the psychotherapist.

THE DUALITY OF THE CLIENT-CENTRED THERAPIST IN THE MEDICAL MODEL SETTING

In accordance with the principle of complementarity, the client-centred therapist lives a sort of 'double life' when working in a medical model setting. From the moment a client crosses the doorstep to his consultation room, the therapist sees the world from within the frame of reference of the client. When the therapy session is over, the therapist is back in a world where the dominating frame of reference is that of the medical model. Because of the seemingly antithetical elements of client-centred therapy and the medical model, these two worlds cannot be integrated into one. The therapist has no other option than to go back and forth between these two very different worlds in the same way that the physicist shuffles back and forth, as he himself chooses, between seeing the electron as a particle and seeing it as a wave, since there is no possibility of seeing them as both at the same time. This is not always easy, and in the following paragraphs I'll describe some of the difficulties, and some of the ways to overcome these difficulties which have been fruitful in my own experience. The main point is to simultaneously protect the therapy process and respect the therapist's 'contract' with the medical model. The crucial issue here is to avoid identifying with either the client or the setting, i.e. to avoid becoming an advocate or message deliverer of the client in relation to the medical model setting and to avoid becoming an advocate or message deliverer of the medical model setting in relation to the client.

The primary responsibility of the client-centred therapist is to protect the therapy process. The therapy process is a delicate process, developing in its own pace and in its own ways, and it has to be protected from the robust, goal-directed and often hurried life of the psychiatric context. This has several practical consequences as follows.

First, the therapist has to refuse to accommodate certain requests from the medical model staff which seem perfectly natural to them. The therapist says 'no' when he is asked to evaluate the client's condition in his next session with the client. Staff members may want this evaluation to assist them in making all sorts of decisions, and it is second nature for them, and part of their job, to make (diagnostic) evaluations when relating with clients; it is expected of them and they expect it of others. It can be difficult for non-informed staff members to understand and respect that the client-centred therapist can have no plans or intentions of any kind when he meets his client. The therapist can also be asked to talk certain things over with the client or deliver a message, and, again, the client-centred therapist refuses to accommodate these requests in order not to have any agenda for his session with the client other than trying to empathically understand the client from the client's own frame of reference. Jerold Bozarth (1990, p. 63) puts it well when he writes that,

The therapist goes with the client — goes at the client's pace — goes with the client in his/her own ways of thinking, of experiencing, of processing. The therapist cannot be up to other things, have other intentions without violating the essence of client-centred therapy. To be up to other things — whatever they might be — is a 'yes but' reaction to the essence of the approach.

Second, the therapist also refuses to let himself be delayed from keeping a therapy appointment on time by drawn-out staff meetings and the like, and he does not allow therapy sessions to be interrupted. This is such an evident responsibility for the therapist, but respect for the client's time is not always taken for granted in the medical model. Sometimes the pressure to take this responsibility less seriously can be quite strong and the therapist must fight for his right to put a higher priority on respecting the client's time than on respecting the setting's time priorities.

Third, the therapist refuses to participate in meetings or conferences about, or with one of, his clients if he thinks his participation can have negative consequences for the therapeutic process with this client. The full psychiatric treatment of the hospitalised patient involves all sorts of meetings: ward meetings for all staff and patients in the ward, meetings with relatives of the patient (with or without the patient himself participating), meetings with staff from other institutions to co-ordinate treatment plans (again with or without the patient himself participating), etc. This is a delicate point and sometimes difficult for the therapist to decide on: will his participation place him in the role of the powerfully influential expert on what is best for the client, in the eyes of the client, or in the eyes of himself, and others, to the detriment of the therapy process?

Many years ago, I routinely participated in the weekly ward meetings for all staff and patients in the ward, until a therapy client of mine discontinued therapy after having witnessed my firm refusal to accommodate the requests of another, very persistent, patient who also participated in the meeting. After this experience, I have consistently refused to participate in this kind of ward meeting.

As to the second kind of meetings (with relatives, or with staff from other institutions), I normally only meet with relatives and 'external' staff if they want my participation as a facilitator for themselves, with their own process with the client. I refuse to meet with them if I am expected to tell them, as an expert, what is wrong with the client, and what is the best way to 'put him right'. If this is their expectation, I refer them to my client's psychiatrist. This is no different from my practice of consultation/supervision/facilitation with 'internal' staff members with respect to their own processes with clients, whether these are therapy clients of mine or not. The significant point, guiding the therapist's decisions on this issue, is that he shall not take on the role of expert on what will be best for the client in any context whatsoever.

Fourth, the client-centred therapist does not accept 'secret' information about his client. This can be a problem with relatives. With the best of intentions, relatives of clients often want to give staff members information about a patient which they deem important when considering the treatment of the patient. At the same time, though, they want it to be kept secret from the patient, not only what the information is about, but also that information actually has been shared. It is normal routine for most other professionals in the medical model setting to listen to such information, even if relatives request that the patient is not told about it. Such is not the case with the client-centred therapist: when relatives contact him, he has to inform them at the outset that he can have no secrets with them about his clients, that he has to feel free to inform the client about this contact according to his own judgement. This is normally accepted, but in rare cases it is not, and relatives can become quite angry with the therapist and threaten to complain to the manager of the therapist. This has to be endured and hopefully the manager of the therapist understands and respects this position. Being given secret information about the client by relatives is tantamount to running the risk of ruining the therapy process because the therapist has made himself a hostage of the relatives: he can no longer feel fully free in his relationship with his client. (This is a frequent issue of discussion among other staff members, too, but because their tasks with patients are different from those of the client-centred therapist, they rarely take as clear a standpoint on this issue as the therapist does.)

Another point pertinent to this issue is, of course, that the therapist can make absolutely no use of such information anyway, since his sole intention with clients is empathic understanding and responding from the client's frame of reference. Any information extraneous to the client's momentary frame of reference is irrelevant to the therapist. The therapist's prompt refusal to receive secret information from relatives is in order not to mislead relatives into thinking that their information is useful for the therapist, and for the sake of the therapist's credibility in the eyes of the client, who would have good reason not to trust the therapist's commitment to confidentiality if he discovered that secret talks had taken place between his relatives and the therapist.

Fifth, the therapist must be careful with his sharing of information and opinions about his therapy clients in the regular staff meetings and conferences, which he normally participates in as part of his work. The main point is not to say anything that others may inadvertently and unbeknownst to themselves use — with the best of intentions — in their relationship with the client in ways that may harm the therapy process. It is useful to imagine what would happen if a staff member said to the client: 'I know from your therapist that …' It is also useful to have as a rule of thumb that, when in doubt, it is better to say too little than too much. This is a delicate point, too; decisions on what to relate and what to keep back are not always easy to make as they depend on a multitude of factors specific to the given situation and the given moment. Most important among these, I think, is the relationship between the therapist and other staff: do they know and appreciate each other? Do they know, trust, and respect the professional characteristics of each other's work? To the degree that this is the case, to the same degree can the therapist, according to my experience, accommodate other staff members' requests for information from the therapy.

A major exception to this concerns written information: the therapist, working within a medical model, will often be obliged to make notes of his work in records and he will not know who gets access to these records in the future. It is therefore advisable to write as little as possible in records. In my experience, it mostly suffices to note that a session has taken place and when the next session is scheduled. It can happen, though, that the client gives information to the therapist in a session, and that this information will be needed by other staff members to do their job. Information of this kind has to be passed on to the relevant staff members as part of the therapist's 'contract' with the medical model setting. This, however, is usually better accomplished in direct dialogue than by using the record. An example of this is given in the section about psychotically depressed clients (see p. 59).

A consequence of the above statement is that the client-centred therapist working in the medical model setting of a psychiatric hospital can not guarantee his client full confidentiality with respect to other staff members. The client is in the hospital because he needs the help, care, and treatment of several professional disciplines. For this to succeed optimally, practitioners of these disciplines must work together, which is only possible if there are no *formal* limits to what they can talk about. This may seem contradictory to the above statement about the importance of the therapist being careful with sharing information from the therapy with other staff members in order to protect the process of therapy but mostly it is not. In reality, very little information of the kind other staff members need to do their work surfaces in therapy sessions, and in my experience it has never been the kind of information that cannot be shared with other staff members without harming the therapy process irreversibly. Some clients ask about this and I tell them that I cannot guarantee full confidentiality in relation to other staff members. I give examples of the kind of information that I will find it necessary to pass on according to my own judgement. This is information about suicidal plans and information that the client takes other medication (or drugs), or takes it in a way that is different from that prescribed by his psychiatrist. In my experience, these are the only two areas where I've sometimes found it necessary, as a consequence of my contract with the medical model, to pass on information to other staff members, whether my client accepts it or not. Fortunately, these occasions are extremely rare. First, staff members on the ward usually know about these things anyway. Second, clients generally know and expect that staff members, including the therapist, will talk together about them, that it is the obligation of hospital staff to do what they can to prevent suicide among in-patients, and that psychiatrists depend on reliable information about the clients' medicine and drug intake to monitor the psychopharmacological treatment. It is important to note, though, that the client-centred therapist does not always (and in my experience very rarely) pass on this kind of information; the point is that the therapist must feel free to do so according to his own judgement.

However seldom it has occurred, though, I've particularly found the decision to pass on information that my client is suicidal very hard to make because of the possibility that more or less coercive interventions will be made towards my client to prevent him from committing suicide. I have the experience of being in a real dilemma between the client-centred and the medical model on this issue, a dilemma I have not been able to resolve for myself with the help of the principle of complementarity; a dilemma where I feel that the client-centred therapist cannot live a 'double life'. I shall therefore discuss this point more extensively in the section about psychotically depressed clients, where the risk of suicide is greatest (see p. 59).

To sum up about the issue of sharing information: the therapist does not share information from the therapy with other staff members if he thinks that this may have harmful consequences for the therapy process. On the other hand, he does not stay silent if he feels this to be against his own ethical standards and contrary to his contract with the medical model. This is an example of the fact that the limits of the medical model setting, within which he is employed, are also the limits of the therapist. More will be said about this in a later section (see p. 55). Finally, other staff members only very rarely need information from the psychotherapy sessions to do their own work and the therapist only very rarely needs information from other treatment modalities to do his work. Therefore, in practice, the sharing of information between the therapist and other staff members, which is needed for truly good reasons, is minimal.

Another consequence of protecting the therapy process is that the therapist does not try to control the way other staff members treat his therapy clients. The therapist offers the professionals in the medical model the same respect which he expects them to offer him. The therapist is aware that the client is in hospital because psychotherapy alone — or, for that matter, psychopharmacological medication, or any other single treatment modality, alone — is not sufficient to help the client optimally. The therapist is also aware that he is deeply dependent on other staff members within the psychiatric setting to do the necessary caring, managing and limit-setting for the client. This is a factor which contributes much to make it possible for the therapist to engage himself fully in the psychotherapeutic relationship with the client. However, the therapist, being dedicated to the philosophy of client-centred theory, will probably sometimes feel that the professionals of the medical model treat a client of his with little respect and understanding and he can feel tempted to try to protect the client by trying to change the ways in which other staff members treat his client. Trying to do this is a mistake: first, it amounts to identification with the client — the client must, after all, find his own way of dealing with his world and protect himself in it, including the world of the medical model. (Would the therapist contact his client's mother, for example, to try to influence her to treat his client with more respect and understanding?) Second, what seems disrespectful or insensitive to the therapist may not seem so to the client. Third, trying to change the way that others behave towards his client implies that the therapist regards himself as the expert on what is best for his client, which is quite antithetical to client-centred theory and risks ruining the therapy process. Protecting the client and protecting the therapy process are two very different, sometimes even mutually exclusive, endeavours.

Example: Protecting the therapy process

Just one example will be given here, which illustrates some of the points explained above. More will be found intermittently in the therapy excerpts and vignettes given later in the book to illustrate therapy processes with psychiatric clients. (Note: throughout the therapy examples, I have made factual changes to the original case material to protect client confidentiality and anonymity, and I believe the examples, as they stand, are beyond personal recognition. On the other hand, there is nothing unrealistic about the factual content of the examples: they faithfully depict the variations of experience of the clients of psychiatry. The reality might just as well have been the reality of the examples. The processes depicted in the examples are true to reality.)

Marion is 30 years old, married, with a five-year-old son. She has been admitted to hospital on her own initiative because of frequent psychotic episodes where she hears voices ordering her to stab, variously, her husband, her son, and herself to death. She is treated with medicine, which she feels helps her, and she has started psychotherapy. She has also started going home for the weekends, but this occasions an upsurge of symptoms. In the therapy, she hesitatingly begins to express very negative feelings towards her husband. This is a change from the first sessions, where she mostly talked about her voices and her fear of giving in to them. In the ward, too, staff members have an impression of problems at home, because of the decline in her condition after weekends, because her husband never visits her, and because she tries to foreshorten her weekend passes, telling her primary nurse that she is a burden on her husband when she is at home. He must take care to keep knives locked away from her, he must do all the cooking and other work in the kitchen because it involves the use of knives, and he must not leave her alone.

Her condition and treatment are discussed in the regular, weekly, staff conference, and the following dialogue evolves between the chief psychiatrist of the ward (CP) and the therapist (T):

CP: I really think we can't get further in the treatment of Marion without some sort of couples therapy. As it is now, I can't imagine her out of hospital in the foreseeable future, and we have many patients on the waiting list. (Turning to T): What about you having some couple sessions with Marion and her husband?

T: I'll gladly do that, if Marion wants me to.

CP: OK, then, you talk with her about that and we can see how it progresses.

T: Oh, no, wait a minute. I'll not introduce this idea or any other to her — you know I only work with issues that she brings up herself.

CP (smiling): Sorry, I forgot for a minute that you have this peculiarity. Then I'll propose it to her and suggest that she brings it up with you, if that is OK with you?

T: Sure, that's fine with me.

Two days later Marion (M) comes for her ordinary session and immediately brings up the subject of couples sessions.

M: CP said to me that it would be a good idea if I brought Douglas (her husband) along to some talks with you.

T: Um hm … (a short silence)

M: But I don't know …

T: You are not sure it would be such a good idea?

M: No … I know I've told you that there are some things about Douglas that make me furious sometimes, but he also helps me a lot, and … I don't know … I don't feel like sitting here telling him about these things. I am sure it would make him feel bad, and I'd understand that, I'd feel bad if he gave me a scolding in front of a stranger, too.

T: You feel sort of disloyal at the thought of bringing him here for a scolding — he doesn't deserve that because you also appreciate his helping you so much?

M: Yes, disloyal, and I'd also feel ashamed, as a coward — I should talk all these things over with him when we are by ourselves. It's just so difficult because he doesn't like to talk about that kind of thing.

Marion continues to discuss various aspects of her problems with her husband and decides that she will not bring her husband with her to a session. She prefers to try to find a way to have a talk with her husband at home about the way she experiences their relationship. Then she turns to the therapist:

M: Will you tell CP that I won't bring Douglas in, explain it to him?
T: For some reason you'd rather have me do it than do it yourself?
M: Yes, I'm afraid he'll be annoyed with me, because I won't bring Douglas in, but I'm sure he'd respect it if you told him.
T: Takes courage to say no to CP?
M: It sure does — I'm afraid he'll dismiss me from hospital soon, if I don't accept his proposal, so will you tell him?
T: You think that if I tell him, he won't dismiss you so soon?
M: Yes ... Oh, why should that make a difference ... It's just that sometimes it is a little difficult to talk with CP, he always seems to be in a hurry, a little impatient, and that makes me nervous. So I'd appreciate it if you would talk with him?
T: You tend to feel nervous with CP, because you feel pressured when he seems to be in a hurry, and you'd prefer to avoid that by having me talk with him?
M: Yes, but ... Well, I ought to do it myself; I'll talk with him myself.
T: You feel an obligation to do it yourself?
M (laughing): Yes, and I'm also a little annoyed with you, because I think you won't do it, but then I also just thought that this is the kind of situation I always try to avoid, saying no to others, and particularly to authorities, and it doesn't do me any good in the long run.

Marion spends the rest of the session coming to terms with her annoyance with me and preparing how best to tell CP about her decision not to have couples sessions. She is transferred to day-patient status two weeks later and after a month or so as a day-patient she is dismissed from hospital altogether. She continues with the psychotherapy as an outpatient, and for a while, she also continues to see CP, concerning questions of medicine, until this aspect of her treatment is transferred to her GP. Her psychotic symptoms have almost disappeared, she has managed to engage her husband in talks about their relationship, and, generally, things are going much better at home. Currently the most frequent theme in her therapy sessions is her fear of being alone.

Comments
1. The dialogue from the staff conference is typical of the therapist's work to avoid getting into situations with his clients where he will be the directive expert. The therapist avoids becoming an advocate

and message deliverer of the medical model to his client. Such situations occur in countless variations and disguises.

2. When the chief psychiatrist mentions the possibility of couples sessions during the staff conference, the therapist has a hunch, from his sessions with the client, that the client will not like this idea. The therapist, though, sees no point in speaking about this hunch, because he also wants to avoid acting as an advocate and message deliverer of the client to the professionals of the medical model. He does not try to influence the psychiatrist, respecting that the psychiatrist will make the most constructive choice possible for him from his frame of reference, which, among other things, also includes balancing the needs, as experienced, of hospitalised patients with the needs of patients on the waiting list.

3. Points 1 and 2 illustrate the 'double life' of the therapist. Further, the client's process in the therapy hopefully illustrates how harmful it would have been if the therapist had either suggested couples sessions to the client (on behalf of the medical model), or suggested to the psychiatrist that couples sessions might not be beneficial (on behalf of the client).

4. The therapy excerpt is also a comment on the question of accommodating client requests. In this instance, the client is very well motivated for psychotherapeutic work, the therapist has a sense of a solid contact and 'working alliance' between him and his client, and he continuously experiences the inner frame of reference of the client — he has a sense of what is going on in the client. This allows him to stay comfortably in the empathic understanding process, even when the client puts a question to him and thereby directs him to his own frame of reference. This, in turn, allows the client to deepen her level of experience and express it (her annoyance with the therapist, her avoidant tendencies), and finally decide to muster her courage and confront the psychiatrist herself. However, the client might just as well have been reluctant and much less self-expressive, and the therapist's sense of the client's voluntary participation might have been much more fragile and fluctuating. In this case, the therapist would be more inclined to answer the question and then try to empathically understand the client's reaction to his answer. (Examples of this are given in some of the therapy excerpts later in the book.) Hospitalised patients often ask the therapist to talk on their behalf to other professionals. When I do answer this question, I normally just explain that I never do this because it is important for me not to confuse my particular relationship with them with other things. This mostly suffices, and I will then try to empathically

understand the patients' reaction to my refusal to accommodate their request.

5. The psychiatrist hinting at the 'peculiarity' of the therapist is probably rather characteristic for a client-centred therapist, compared with therapists from other orientations, who would more willingly introduce issues from their own frame of reference in their sessions with clients. The client-centred therapist's dedication to safeguard the client's freedom and autonomy in the therapy process, and the importance this therapist attaches to the locus of initiative resting firmly with the client in their relationship, is rarely fully understood outside of client-centred circles. It can therefore seem a superfluous and roundabout procedure to other professionals when they (like CP, in the example) must, themselves, address the client to propose that the client talks something over with the therapist, which the therapist is perfectly willing to discuss with the client in the first place.

The essence of the six main issues that have been dealt with in this chapter about the duality of the client-centred therapist's work can be summed up as follows:

- The therapy must progress in parallel, not integrated, with the medical model treatments; those two worlds must be kept separate, not mixed together.

- In his relations with the client, the therapist must take care not to identify with, or become the advocate or message deliverer of, the medical model, or of the staff members who are also his colleagues.

- In his relations with other staff members, the therapist must take care not to identify with, or become the advocate or message deliverer of, the client.

- The therapist listens to the client's experiences with the medical model, and with other staff members, as respectfully and acceptantly as he listens to any other of the client's experiences.

- The therapist listens to other staff members' experiences with his clients as respectfully and acceptantly as he listens to any other of the staff members' experiences.

Dave Mearns (1994, pp. 53–6) has stressed the importance of the therapist being 'beside' the client, not 'on the side of' the client. This is, to me, a very important point to stress, and, when working in a psychiatric context, it is equally important to be 'beside' the psychiatric context, but not 'on the side of' this context. The concept of complementarity is often helpful in this respect.

Alternatively stated: the therapist must remain the client's client-centred therapist, and no more than the client's client-centred therapist, throughout. The service he offers clients is acceptant empathic understanding, none other.

All this is much easier said than done. The therapist can sometimes feel quite split when he passes back and forth between the world of therapy sessions and the world of the medical model: there is so little of his experiences in one world that he can use or share in the other. He can sometimes feel disloyal to his client, because he participates in 'medical model talk' about his client with other staff members and does nothing to make them understand his client from the client's frame of reference. Likewise, he can feel disloyal to his colleagues because he listens with empathic understanding to his client's (negative) experiences of them in therapy sessions and does nothing to correct the client's impression in accordance with his own experiences of his colleagues. It is again useful in this situation to think of the principle of complementarity: both worlds are true but when in one you cannot see the other and vice versa.

However helpful the principle of complementarity may be to dissolve many potential dilemmas of the therapist, it is of paramount importance that the therapist has access to a 'third world': a world of his own. There must be at least one person with whom the therapist can talk freely about all of his experiences, from his own frame of reference, with absolutely no risk to either the therapy process or to his contract with the medical model. This person would preferably be another client-centred therapist who is knowledgeable about, or working within, the medical model setting. The therapist's need for somebody to pay attention to, and try to understand, his experiences from his own frame of reference has to be met frequently to counter feelings of isolation with the concomitant risk of 'burnout'. The ideal solution is a small peer consultation or supervision group that meets regularly. If this need is adequately met, the above-mentioned difficulties are more than compensated for by the richness, depth and diversity of experiences of the client-centred therapist working in the medical model setting of, for example, a psychiatric hospital.

THE ROLE OF THE CLIENT-CENTRED THERAPIST IN STAFF CONFERENCES

In the preceding section it was stated that other staff members very rarely need information from the therapy to do their own work and the therapist very rarely needs information about the client's other treatments to do his work. This, of course, is because client-centred therapy concerns itself exclusively with understanding from within the client's frame of reference in the here-and-now. It is a heuristic/ phenomenological approach, whereas other treatment modalities build on an external frame of reference in relation to the client, i.e. on the diverse explanatory theories of the medical/biological science, of nursing, of occupational therapy, etc. Nevertheless, professionals within these treatment modalities also try to take into account the frame of reference of the patients, and they try to respect the patients' wishes and requests. For example, the concept of 'informed consent' is important for these professionals.

Professionals from other treatment modalities depend on exchanging information about their diverse observations of clients to do their job; psychiatrists, for example, depend heavily on the observations of nurses in their process of diagnosing, and subsequently deciding on which psychopharmacological treatment to offer to the client. The staff conference, where such information is exchanged and where decisions on how to proceed with the treatment of the patients are made, is therefore central to the work of almost everybody in the hospital and central to the 'fate' of the patients during their stay in hospital.

But the work of the client-centred therapist is not dependent on exchanging information with other professionals and vice versa, so it can be very legitimately asked: 'what is the role of the client-centred therapist in the staff conference?'

In my opinion, the answer is: 'there is no role for the client-centred therapist in the staff conference'. Not with respect to his therapy with his clients, at least.

I have worked, as mentioned already, for more than 25 years in a psychiatric hospital, many of these without participating in staff conferences, and this was inconsequential as far as my therapeutic work was concerned. It was not inconsequential, however, for my personal feeling of well-being in my work. I came to feel more and more isolated and estranged from most of my colleagues: I might as well have had my consultation room far away from the hospital, as an occasional telephone contact was sufficient to exchange the necessary information between the staff members of the client's ward and myself. Therefore, for my own sake, I started to participate in the staff conferences of the two wards for which I did most of my work, with the intention of finding out whether I might have a contribution to make in this setting. It became apparent that this was the case, and in the following section I'll describe the contribution that I, as a client-centred therapist, or, more correctly in this context, a person-centred practitioner, could make to the staff conference.

As a member of the staff conference group, with no agenda of my own, I found that I could be helpful by facilitating the spontaneous tendencies towards a person-centred approach that already existed in the group, especially among the nurses. Although a holistic view of the patients is a commonly accepted value of nursing, and although most nurses have an intuitive feeling that listening to their patients is part of good nursing, many feel that they are 'doing nothing' when they are 'just listening'. In addition, nurses often do not fully realise how important their relationship with their patients is: that their ability to create a good relationship with their patients is of primary therapeutic importance and not secondary to, for example, psychopharmacological treatment and psychotherapy or, even worse, irrelevant to the outcome of treatment. Nurses often welcome the great value which the client-centred therapist attaches to empathic listening and understanding and to the quality of the relationship with the patient, and can feel supported and strengthened by the therapist's interest in this aspect of their work.

More specifically, I could be facilitative of the person-centred tendencies of the staff conference group by my interest in translating a categorising and diagnosing language into a language of concrete and individualised characteristics of relationships. This could be the case, for example, if mention is made of a patient's narcissism. What does this mean in terms of nurses' daily relationships with the patient in the ward? Further, what does it mean that the client is 'unmotivated' or 'withdrawn' or 'psychotic', etc.? Such questions underline the importance of the quality of staff members' relationships with patients and support staff members' tendency to deal with and talk about patients as human beings alongside their obligations to deal with and talk about them as containers of different diseases.

I could also be facilitative of the person-centred tendencies of the staff conference group by my interest in the patients' points of view, i.e. by using appropriate occasions to ask: 'what does the patient himself want? Does anybody know what the patient will feel and think about this? These thoughts you have about the patient's problems: are they yours or are they the patient's?' Treatment plans with quite far-reaching consequences for patients are sometimes discussed in staff conferences, and most nurses welcome the above kinds of questions because they create a space for them to speak with the patient's voice, which they are most often very familiar with from their day-long contacts with patients in the ward. Nurses are most often the persons who know best what treatment plans are acceptable to patients, whether the plans are about changes in the psychopharmacological treatment of patients, changes in their social network, changes in their daily activities, or whatever. In addition, it is most often nurses who will discuss the treatment plans extensively with patients, so it is important to most of them that the plans are reasonably in accordance with patient wishes, and that they will not feel obliged to try, more or less subtly, to enforce treatment plans on patients.

Further, I could enhance the importance attached to empathic understanding by using nurses' accounts and descriptions of patients to guess at one or several ways the patient might be understood empathically. This facilitates nurses' spontaneous tendency to try to understand their patients empathically.

Finally, I could facilitate staff members' spontaneous liking and sympathy for their patients, quite simply by listening with interest and acceptance to expressions of these feelings, and by expressing my own liking and sympathy for my clients openly. These attitudes are often regarded with a little suspicion in psychiatry because of the prizing of 'objectivity' in this discipline, although neither staff nor patients thrive well with this effort at pure 'objectivity'. It is often a relief for staff members to allow themselves to like their patients. All too often, staff members in psychiatry lean backwards in a somewhat distancing attitude so as not to risk being regarded as subjective or as identifying with clients. Rogers (1961, p. 52) wrote:

> 'We are afraid that if we let ourselves freely experience these positive feelings toward another we may be trapped by them … So as a reaction, we tend to build up distance between ourselves and others — aloofness, a 'professional' attitude, an impersonal relationship … It is a real achievement when we can learn, even in certain relationships or at certain times in those relationships, that it is safe to care, that it is safe to relate to the other as a person for whom we have positive feelings.'

It is important that avoidance of identification with the patient is not confused with a distancing attitude that puts a taboo on the liking of patients.

This role of mine, at staff conferences, has contributed to the wards becoming, in general, more 'person-centred' in the daily interactions between staff and patients. In addition, it has helped me out of my feelings of isolation and invisibility among all the other employees in the hospital. A pre-condition for this to happen is, of course, that the person in charge of the staff conference, typically a psychiatrist, i.e. a representative of the medical model, is sufficiently broad-minded to allow space and time for it. To the degree that this is the case, staff conferences can develop into a very exciting and enriching dialogue between the medical model and the person-centred approach.

I think most client-centred therapists working in a medical model setting will recognise this feeling of their psychotherapeutic work being (and having to be) separated, isolated, and almost invisible from all the activity of the rest of the setting. Some therapists may prefer to live with this 'invisibility' of their therapeutic work. For others, though, 'living with it' may entail a risk of 'burnout' that has to be avoided by becoming visible in the setting, in some way or another, in spite of the 'invisibility' of their work with clients. This absolute independence between client-centred therapy and the treatment modalities of the medical model setting has to be respected, though, no matter to what degree the therapist chooses to interact with the representatives of the medical model. Furthermore, this independence seems to me to be exclusive to client-centred therapy as compared to other modes of psychotherapy. Both psychoanalytic psychotherapy and cognitive-behavioural therapy, for example, will use information from the psychiatric setting in the psychotherapy. In staff conferences, furthermore, psychotherapists from these schools of therapy will contribute with information from the therapy that may be useful for other professionals in the setting. It may even be the case that nurses, for example, are expected to adapt their contact with clients according to the information they receive from the psychotherapist, i.e. the nurses' work is subordinate to the psychotherapy. This difference between client-centred therapy and other schools of therapy has to do, of course, with client-centred therapy being exclusively phenomenological, it has to do with the client-centred therapist not being the expert on the client, and it has to do with the egalitarian philosophy of client-centred theory.

HELPING THE HELPERS AND TAKING CARE OF THE CARETAKERS

Another role which can help make the client-centred therapist feel less invisible in the setting, and which is of great importance in its own right, is that of 'helper to the helpers' or 'caretaker of the caretakers'.

Nurses working in psychiatric wards, and particularly in closed psychiatric wards, are exposed to unusually high levels of emotional intensity, and to unusually bewildering behaviours, during almost the whole of their working day. Episodes with outbursts of violence, whether directed towards others, towards the person himself, or towards material objects, are frequent too. This is, of course, a constant strain and toll on nurses' own psychological resources, and the way they are exposed to, and must interfere with, different kinds and degrees of violence, often has an impact on them that can only be described as traumatic.

It is important, therefore, that nurses themselves, as well as administrators, recognise that it is often not possible for them to process all these experiences, on their own, during a normally very busy working day. First, they simply haven't got the time to take care of themselves, in the midst of taking care of the patients and all that that entails. Second, they will normally all be so 'filled up' with their own experiences that they are unable to listen very well to each other. Planned 'time out' and an external facilitator is most often necessary to counter the risk of 'burnout' among nurses, as well as the risk of high turnover of staff, and the risk of nurses' behaviour rigidifying into defensive routine strategies with the patients.

The approach of the client-centred therapist — non-directive, non-diagnostic, and universally applicable as it is — is eminently suited to help nurses 'survive' in a psychologically healthy way, i.e. to learn and develop from their experiences, rather than being, perhaps, harmed by them. The therapist, therefore, should not only work with the patients, but also with the nurses (and sometimes doctors and others as well), in group 'debriefing' sessions, and/or in individual 'crisis therapy' sessions. This work is not much different from ordinary client-centred therapy. The only difference, in my practice of it, is that I structure group sessions to make sure that everyone has time to talk and be listened to and understood, and I do not allow a short run of individual crisis sessions to turn into more long-term, personal therapy. This is partly because of my own time schedule, and partly because I do not wish to enter into a close, long-term therapy relationship with individuals whom I also meet every day as colleagues and friends. Apart from a few crisis sessions, I would doubt my ability to consistently 'keep out of the client's way', if the client was a near colleague and/or friend of mine.

Besides the importance of this kind of work for staff members themselves, and the way it makes the therapist feel more visible in his work setting, it also supports the therapist's confidence in his own competence. It is very rewarding work in the sense that these well-functioning 'clients' very quickly experience the positive results of it. This is helpful as an antidote to sometimes diminishing morale in the work with psychotic clients, where the therapist, from time to time, can doubt if more noticeable, positive results will ever come about.

THE LIMITS OF THE SETTING ARE THE THERAPIST'S LIMITS

Depending on the specifics of the actual medical model setting in question, there will probably be some limits to the work of the client-centred therapist in this setting, which the therapist must come to terms with in one way or another and which make the work different from, for example, the private practitioner's work.

One has already been mentioned: the therapist cannot guarantee his client total confidentiality. The therapist must feel free to share information with other staff members according to his own judgement, because the treatment of the hospitalised, psychiatric patient is basically a team job. If the therapist feels wholly antagonistic towards this, he should probably not work in a medical model setting, at least not as extreme a medical model setting as the psychiatric hospital.

Another potential limit is the therapist's more or less intimate knowledge of staff members who are also important people in the lives of his clients, at least for the duration of hospitalisation. Some staff members may be very close colleagues of the therapist; they may even be close friends, and this can pose a threat to the therapist's ability to avoid identification with these staff members when a client is exploring his experiences with them. It has happened once in my career that I identified so much with a colleague of mine, who felt very tormented and harassed by the behaviour of my client, that I felt disqualified as this client's therapist and terminated the therapy. I see this as a therapeutic failure of mine, but also as an example of an aspect of the work that is harder in a hospital setting than in private practice, for example. In the hospital setting, the therapist has not only to avoid identification with his clients but also with his colleagues, however close to the therapist they may be.

Other limits will probably be more varying according to the specific setting, so I'll just give one further example from my own work as follows.

Some of my clients come from the closed ward of the hospital where I work. The main purpose of their treatment in this ward is to better their condition in a way that makes it possible to transfer them to an open ward as quickly as possible. This, however, may be an open ward where I do not work, so normally I cannot promise clients from the closed ward that I will continue therapy with them after transfer; another therapist will do that. This does not change the way I work with these clients; I try to empathically understand their experiences of this limit, as of anything else, and I accommodate requests to ease my client's transfer to another therapist if I can. Sometimes I make an exception to this 'rule', but not very often, because that would be a sure way to build up a case overload. However, this limit is the one I experience as the most difficult one to tolerate in my work. It is often with a feeling of sadness and regret (sometimes shared with the client, sometimes not), that I take leave of a client from the closed ward when he is ready for transfer to an open ward where I do not work.

In addition, it is worth repeating that it is of course crucial that the limits of the setting are not so narrow that they become an insurmountable hindrance for client-centred therapy to take place at all. This means basically that the decisions the therapist makes to protect the therapy process, as described above, are respected. If this is not the case, client-centred therapy cannot take place in that setting. The most central point, and the hardest point, too, for the setting to respect, is, in my experience, that the therapist is not a better expert on the client than the client himself. If the therapist is requested to be an expert on his client, in spite of having done his best to avoid it, he will probably have to stop doing client-centred therapy in that setting or leave his job to do client-centred therapy in a more broad-minded setting.

Finally, it goes without saying that the setting must work in ways that are reasonably ethically compatible with the therapist. Fortunately, the situation portrayed in the film 'One Flew Over the Cuckoo's Nest' seems to belong to the past in most psychiatric contexts.

I have been lucky to work in a medical model setting with a spirit of great openness and broad-mindedness and in such a setting the therapist may experience advantages that are not found in other settings. This will be the subject of the next section.

ADVANTAGES OF WORKING IN THE MEDICAL MODEL
SETTING OF A PSYCHIATRIC HOSPITAL

One advantage of working in a psychiatric hospital is the opportunity it gives the client-centred therapist to work with a very rich variety of clients. The psychiatric hospital normally has in-patients, patients in day care, and outpatients. Some outpatients have been in the hospital and are in follow-up treatment; others start and finish as outpatients without becoming in-patients at any time. This means that the therapist has the opportunity to work with clients along the whole continuum from the most withdrawn and least self-expressive to psychologically rather well adjusted, self-expressive crisis clients. This also entails the possibility of experiencing both very short-term therapy and very long-term therapy, and working with couples and families in addition to individuals.

Another advantage is the philosophical questions that confront the client-centred therapist in the psychiatric hospital. The work with psychotic clients raises questions as to the nature of reality. The confrontation with the explanatory models of the setting necessitates thinking about the relation between these and the phenomenological position of the therapist. The frequently made biological explanations of the clients' symptoms necessitate thinking about the relation between biological phenomena and psychological phenomena. Finally, the psychiatric hospital is replete with hard ethical questions and problems. The very existence of involuntarily admitted patients, and of involuntarily treated patients, is the subject of a never-ending ethical discussion. All this is, in my experience, very promoting of the therapist's personal development and 'learning about life', given, of course, that the therapist is open to viewpoints other than his own.

Further, a reasonably open and broad-minded medical model setting can also be a very protected place for the novice therapist to gain experience. This therapist knows in theory that he is not responsible for the client's life, that he is 'only' responsible for creating optimal conditions for the client's growth. In my experience, however, novice therapists will worry whether they should interfere or not, if they experience the client as helpless in one way or another. In the medical model setting, the therapist knows that others take care of this. He can therefore feel more free to work non-directively and slowly develop his own trust in the therapy process, as he experiences, time and again, how clients develop positively, although it often takes a long time and the road can be very tortuous and full of hardships in many diverse ways. Having developed this trust, as an integrated part of himself, the therapist is better equipped to work in the more independent setting of, for example, a private practice.

Another advantage is that the novice therapist is relieved of the potentially complicating problem concerning fees, and other practical arrangements, when working in a medical model setting. In many ways, therefore, the optimal medical model setting is also a setting where the novice therapist can safely gain experience of the practice of client-centred therapy without having also to worry about 'extra-therapeutic' or management problems. This, combined with the variety and depth of experiences mentioned above, makes the open and broad-minded psychiatric hospital an ideal setting for training and starting practising client-centred therapy — on the condition, of course, that good supervision and consultation are available.

Finally, the 'inside' experience gained from having worked in a psychiatric hospital is valuable to the therapist even when no longer working there. Many myths exists about psychiatric hospitals, with and without good reasons, and it may be of value to the therapist to have some more factual knowledge about psychiatry when he and his client consider the possibility that his client might seek psychiatric help. In Denmark, at least, with the way the mental health system is organised here, this might easily happen to a therapist in private practice.

Part Three
Relating with the patients of psychiatry

Patients diagnosed with psychotic depression

Characteristics of the therapy process

The patients who are so depressed that hospitalisation becomes necessary are without energy to do anything, even sometimes without energy to talk about their experience; they are most often totally hopeless and despairing about themselves, their past, and their future. They are a far cry from what the layperson has in mind when he thinks of someone being 'depressed', and they are a far cry from clients treated under the diagnosis of depression in private practices and outpatient clinics. The depressed patients of psychiatry are most often depressed to psychotic degrees; their depressed ideation is delusional.

The different schools of psychotherapy have all been developed with clients outside the psychiatric system, and with the exception of client-centred therapy, they normally demand that the client has some energy available for goal-directed cooperation in the therapeutic process. This, however, cannot be demanded of the depressed client in the psychiatric hospital. In my experience, therefore, the non-demanding, non-directive client-centred therapy is the only suitable psychotherapy for these clients.

This does not mean, though, that the client participates wholeheartedly in the client-centred therapeutic relationship. On the contrary, he often participates half-heartedly, partly seeing no meaning in this activity, as he sees no meaning in any other activity. He is convinced that nothing can be of any help to him, that he is doomed to live in depressed despair for the rest of his life — or commit suicide.

'Sitting through' a depressive episode with the severely depressed client, therefore, demands a lot of the client-centred therapist: he will not experience his client's depression lifting as a consequence of his relationship with the client; session after session passes by with no seeming change in the client's condition. The therapist will not be able to escape feelings of powerlessness, and may be tempted to avoid such feelings by subtly or not so subtly suggesting some 'helpful' activity to the client or by voicing some encouraging comments. Such directive interventions, however, will only serve to alienate the client and deepen the client's sense of isolation and self-blame, and it will reinforce the client's own tendency to blame himself for not 'pulling himself together' and not 'looking at the bright side' of his life. The only thing that can help the therapist tolerate this feeling of powerlessness is his knowledge, from earlier experiences, that some day the depression will lift, suddenly or more slowly over time, but it will lift — nobody stays in that condition forever. When this happens the formerly depressed client will often tell the therapist how much less anxious and isolated he felt in his depression when, in sessions, the therapist stayed (psychologically) close to him, and how this was important for the client feeling able to 'pull through'. The therapist will have no knowledge about the extent to which the therapy helped effect the sometimes miraculously seeming change in the client that sets in when the depression lifts. Depressions are known to lift by themselves in time, and anti-depressive medicine is shown by most research to be of importance in shortening the depressive episode, but the role of client-centred therapy is, to the best of my knowledge, unknown. There seems to be little doubt that biological factors are important in explaining these severe depressions, but this does not detract from the fact that client-centred therapy, in the experience of clients, at least eases and ameliorates their progress through the depression.

It is also the case that 'sitting through' a depressive episode with a client deepens the relationship with the client and makes it more likely that the client will want, and benefit from, therapy, after the depression has lifted. Without psychotherapy during the depressive episode, many clients will try to forget all about their depression when it has lifted, and they are the ones who are more likely to be re-admitted with a new episode of depression (or in a manic phase if the client is disposed to react variously with depressive or manic episodes). The experience of client-centred therapy during the depressive episode, though, makes it more likely that a formerly depressed client will want to continue therapy to explore the meaning of his depression and ways to avoid becoming depressed again. Clients who are prone to become depressed seem often to regard themselves positively only when they are happily and actively doing something useful for others, whereas needs to be passive or to do something exclusively for their own pleasure or having 'negative' feelings of sadness, anger, irritation, apprehension, etc., are denied to awareness. Within the safe atmosphere of a client-centred relationship, this denial seems less likely to occur when the depression lifts.

The issue of suicide

In any discussion of therapy with depressed clients, the issue of suicidal risk is essential. Of all psychiatric patients, the risk of suicide is greatest with severely depressed patients. Because most depressed patients in the psychiatric hospital are considered psychotic and because this condition is reversible, hospital staff are obliged by law to take the necessary precautions to prevent these patients committing suicide as a result of a relatively short period with depressed, psychotic ideation. The client-centred therapist is no exception to this.

However, the client-centred therapist will probably experience questions concerning the prevention of suicide as more controversial than other staff members. In the client-centred community, suicide is an often-debated subject. Many feel, as a consequence of being convinced of the existence of the actualising tendency, and as a consequence of trust in the facilitative potential of the core conditions, and because they are motivated by the non-directive attitude, that the client makes the best decisions for himself, including a decision to commit suicide. This, then, also means that a client's decision to commit suicide should not be interfered with. According to client-centred theory, a decision to commit suicide expresses the client's actualisation of his most constructive potential at the moment, whether it is based on what is regarded as psychotic ideation or not. Furthermore, the client-centred therapist will trust the core conditions to facilitate the most constructive change possible in the client, or, in other words, the core conditions will release those potentials within the client that best enable the client to consider all the possibilities, including options other than suicide. The medical model, on the other hand, regards the psychotically depressed patient's decision to commit suicide as a symptom of a predominantly biologically caused, but curable, disease, and the fulfilled suicide as a tragic accident that must be prevented. In my country, Denmark, legislation on involuntary commitment to a psychiatric hospital, and involuntary psychiatric treatment, distinguishes between 'existential' and 'psychotic' suicides, and obliges the personnel of psychiatry to try to prevent the latter. To this end, the application of forceful means (forced transfer to a closed ward and/or forced medication, for example) is legally sanctioned.

Therefore, when a psychotic client of mine discloses suicidal ideation in a session with me, and I know my colleagues in the ward are unaware of this, I feel myself to be in a dilemma: if I keep this information to myself, I do not risk giving occasion for forceful means being applied to my client. This seems to me to be quite antithetical to the philosophy of client-centred therapy to which I am dedicated; it goes against my most deeply held values. Furthermore, I feel rather convinced that a society which does not sanction the use of force within the realm of psychiatry would be a better society. I am not convinced that the goal (keeping people alive) justifies the means (forceful interventions). That, however, is a political standpoint with respect to current legislation, which, in my opinion, should be expressed along the normal channels of democracy and not in decisions concerning individual clients.

If, on the other hand, I decide to tell, I adhere to my contract with the medical model. I take my share of our common obligation to do our best to prevent suicides based on psychotic ideation. It seems so obvious that I should do so, because I have seen so many psychotically depressed clients become almost miraculously better in a relatively short time. The temporality of this condition, the evidence of biological factors being involved, and the evidence of the beneficial effect of medication, seem to leave little doubt that, of course, these clients should be kept alive, forcefully if necessary. The main reason for this would be to gain sufficient time for treatment to effect a change, and this is also what I, as a client-centred therapist, want. I trust the facilitative potential of the core conditions, but I dare not trust that they will facilitate major changes overnight. I am concerned with the finality of suicide; I want my client to come back for his next session; I want a proper chance for the core conditions (and medication) to release the more constructive potential of the client, which I feel convinced is there. Finally, one may understand the fact that many patients express gratitude that they were kept alive, even with forceful means, as still another point in favour of forceful intervention to prevent suicide based on psychotic ideation.

None the less, I feel myself to be in doubt when confronted with this situation. Therefore, when I pass on the information that a psychotic client of mine is suicidal, I do so in opposition to what I'd most deeply wish to be able to do, namely to trust the core conditions to facilitate the most constructive change possible in these clients as I do with all other clients. When I deviate from this, I experience myself as saying, 'yes, but' to the essence of client-centred therapy.

However, in the end I sometimes decide to pass on the information that a psychotically depressed client has disclosed suicidal ideation to me. I am supposed to do this as a consequence of my contract with the medical model, and, if nothing else, I do not want to jeopardise my position on account of this complicated, but rare, dilemma with psychotically suicidal clients. This, though, does not detract from the fact that I find the issue of suicide to be the hardest issue of all to deal with in my work within the psychiatric system; it is the sole issue where I sometimes act according to the medical model in my relationship with a client. Later I shall give my reasons for this kind of interference having become a still more infrequent event in my practice, but first I shall give an example of the dilemmas concerning suicidal risk, where I did interfere with my client's process, thereby placing myself in the role of the expert on what would be best for the client. This example is extended with a typical 'person-centred-approach dialogue' with other staff members involved in the combined treatment of the client.

Example: Psychotic, suicidal ideation and person-centred dialogue with nurses

A psychotically depressed client of mine talks, in her first two sessions with me, about her view of herself as a destructive person, guilty of much evil. For example, she is convinced of her guilt in the atrocities that took place during the civil wars in former Yugoslavia. She is convinced that she will be caught and put to trial in The Hague and convicted for her crimes, and she is also convinced that sooner or later the ward staff will realise her evilness and deliver her over to the court in The Hague, although they repeatedly assure her they will not. A kernel of truth in all this seems to be that she did not support her son's wish to join the Danish military peace force in Yugoslavia, but apart from that, she is evidently delusional when seen from my frame of reference. This does not make any difference, however, in my effort to understand her empathically in my sessions with her.

Then, in her third session with me, she tells me that she is starting to think of suicide as a way to avoid the humiliating trial in The Hague. She has also made concrete plans for how she might kill herself. She would walk to the nearby railway and throw herself in front of the train. She also says that making the driver of the train suffer by this just shows how evil she is and always has been, what she has done has always been destructive to others and now she can find no other sure way to kill herself than by making the driver of the train suffer. That, she says, is just the way she is. During the session, she turned this over and over and came to a point where she said that she did want to kill herself in a sure way but the thought of the train driver maybe coming to feel responsible for having killed her plagued her. At the end of the session she told me that during sessions with me she had started to feel a little better, a little relieved, and this also happened in talks with her two primary nurses. However, when these talks ended, she felt just as despairing as before or even worse, but still, her talks with the nurses and me meant little oases of light to her in a desert of darkness.

After this session, I had some thinking to do. I knew this client had not talked about suicide before and my evaluation was that her suicidal thinking was grounded in temporary, reversible psychotic ideation. She was typically a client whom the psychiatric system is expected to prevent from committing suicide. In addition, because she, until that moment, had been delusional in a quiet, non-destructive way, she was in an open ward from which clients often went out for a stroll in the surrounding park and forest without anybody noticing, so she had ample opportunity to get to the railway tracks.

Should I pass this information on to the staff members of her ward? What would be the consequences of passing it on? Further, if I decided to pass it on, how should I do it?

I wondered about risks to the therapy process. Might she lose confidence in me? Particularly, might she lose confidence in my confidence in her? Might she feel betrayed by me? Might she feel that I had left her isolated in her hell? On the other hand, suicide would be the end of any therapy, which I would find quite tragic, in the light of the likely reversibility of her condition. In spite of her statement, that she had started to feel a little relief in her relationships with me and her primary nurses, I felt I needed more time to become assured that my relationship with her was strong enough to 'hold' her (together with the nurses' relationship with her) and I wouldn't get that time if she killed herself.

What about the consequences for myself? How would I feel if she committed suicide and I hadn't told anyone I knew about her plans? In some way or the other, I felt convinced that it would be a very painful experience. In addition, it would be a great relief for myself to pass on this information, to share the burdensome feelings of worry, doubt, and responsibility with my colleagues in the ward. I also felt that not telling would be a breach of my contract with the medical model system and I did not want to jeopardise my trustworthiness to that system.

In the end, I decided that the consequences of telling would be less negative than the consequences of not telling. I also made this decision, however, with an uneasy feeling of betraying the client-centred philosophy by making myself the expert on the client, because I had decided to take steps to interfere with what the client might find to be the best decision for herself.

Having made this decision, I had to decide which way I wanted to pass on my information. It would be quick and easy to make a note in the records and leave the rest to others, but I did not want to write about any details in the records in order to respect confidentiality to the greatest degree possible. On the other hand, I did want staff members, who were currently responsible for her treatment, to have the necessary details to make their own decisions. In addition, I wanted to do my best to secure that decisions made on the basis of my information would be the best possible decisions for anybody involved.

Therefore, I went to the ward and asked for a talk with the head nurse and the client's primary nurse. They would be the next in line who would feel responsible for decisions made to secure the life of my client. After having told them about my client's plan and about my own thoughts and feelings with respect to her suicidal ideation, I reverted to a person-centred approach in the rest of my talk with the two nurses. The following dialogue took place:

PN (primary nurse): I am not so surprised. Sometimes in our talks the last couple of days, she has seemed a little guarded. I have felt she held something back, had some secret on her mind — I think it must have been her thoughts about suicide.

HN (head nurse): Maybe we ought to call the psychiatrist on duty — he could talk with her and decide what to do ... But the one who is on duty today is new here and he doesn't know her at all — he might transfer her to the closed ward, just in case.

T (therapist): You feel transferring her would be an over-reaction?

HN: Yes, and she (the client) would feel it as a transgression. Somehow, I think we can handle it without a transfer.

PN: I agree. I don't think she is close enough to act on her plans for a transfer to be reasonable. I have the same feeling, that sometimes she sees glimpses of light in her situation, and furthermore, I have not seen her leave the ward — she only goes out to sit on the terrace sometimes in the afternoon, she is mostly in her room.

HN: That's right. Still, she might just suddenly decide to leave.

T: So doing nothing seems too little, and having her transferred seems too much?

HN: Exactly. I think, what I want is for her not to leave the ward without company, to feel sure she doesn't.

T: You would like to feel sure that she'd respect that.

HN: Right. I think we could trust her, if we told her we didn't want her to leave the ward on her own, then she wouldn't, (to PN) don't you think? You know her better than I do?

PN: Oh, yes, I see her as a very trustworthy person. I think that would be the right way to handle it. But what about CP (chief psychiatrist of the ward)?

T: What would he think of this plan?

HN: Yes, I think I'll call him, I think he will approve of this way of doing it. He knows her, too, but he should know about it, and I'd like his confirmation.

PN: I'd like that, too.

HN: So I'll call CP and then we go and talk with her and you (T) tell her what you have told us and we take over from there, talking with her about the way we want to handle it?

T and PN: Fine.

Comments

1. Both in the immediate talk on the ward and in the next regular session, the client expresses mixed feelings about my passing on the

information about her plans to kill herself. She half expected me to do it, though, knowing that in principle all staff, including myself, must feel free to share the information about patients, which they want to share. She feels relieved to have the decision taken off her shoulders, but she also misses the feeling of security it gave her to know that she could end her pains by killing herself.

2. Later, when she is much better, she feels shocked at the thought that she might have lost her life as a result of thinking so unrealistically. On the other hand, she finds it most likely that she would not have tried to kill herself; somehow, there was, at the time, a little hope in her of things getting better, so she is also somewhat disappointed that I didn't have enough confidence in her. However, she understands me very well; she'd have done the same had she been in my shoes; she feels forgiving towards me. All this is expressed in normal client-centred dialogue in sessions around the time when the depression has lifted substantially.

3. It is noteworthy that I did not discuss my decision to pass on information about her suicidal plans with my client. In this instance, I notified my client about it afterwards: sometimes I do it beforehand, but the decision is not up for discussion, although, of course, I'll explain the reasons for my decision if requested to by the client. Decisions like the above are made from my own frame of reference (or from that of the medical model) and furthermore, they are made with a feeling of conviction that discussing them with the client will not make me change my mind. I don't want to deceive the client into thinking that I might change my mind by discussing it, and I don't want to burden the client with my concerns; they are mine, not the client's. Furthermore, I don't want to risk getting into a relationship with the client where he might try to commit himself to me by making promises concerning his future plans of action (promising not to commit suicide, for example). In my opinion, I protect the therapy process better by risking whatever reactions he may have towards my unilateral decision. Finally, I want to revert to my role as a client-centred therapist as soon as possible. The precautions to be taken, if any, as a consequence of my passing on information about a client's suicidal ideation, lie within the realm of responsibility of other staff members, who will discuss the precautions with the client.

4. It is quite typical that I in no way tried to interfere with the decisions made by the two nurses as a consequence of the information I had given them. On the contrary, I tried to help facilitate clarification of their feelings and thoughts about how to proceed. It

would have made no difference if they, on the basis of their experiences, had come to a decision to do nothing at all or had decided to ask for a transfer of the patient to the closed ward. As soon as I have passed on information that a client of mine is seriously suicidal, I want to revert to my role as the client's therapist, i.e. a role where I am in no way an expert on what might be the best for the client. Furthermore, it is my experience that nurses in general, because of their long-time daily contact with patients and their normally relatively humanistic approach to patients, can be trusted to choose very wisely in situations like the one exemplified.

Of course, any client-centred therapist working in a psychiatric hospital has to find his own position concerning the issue of suicide. Rogers (1951, p. 48) had the following to say about this issue:

> Does the counsellor have the right, professionally or morally, to permit a client seriously to consider … suicide as a way out, without making a positive effort to prevent this choice? Is it a part of our general social responsibility that we may not tolerate such thinking or such action on the part of another? These are deep issues, which strike to the very core of therapy. They are not issues which one person can decide for another. Different therapeutic orientations have acted upon different hypotheses. All that one person can do is to describe his own experience and the evidence which grows out of that experience.

Responding to the implicit question in this quotation by Rogers, my own experience has been that, over the years, as my confidence in my competence as a therapist has grown, I increasingly rarely decide to disclose my clients' suicidal ideation and intentions to others. In spite of this, no clients of mine have committed suicide. I have learned that a client's disclosure of plans to commit suicide is still one or more crucial steps away from actually committing suicide. I have also learned to become more trusting of that flicker of hope implicit in the client actually being there with me, and in the client's feeling of reduced isolation and abandonment as a result of my willingness to listen to, and try to understand, his suicidal ideation, although he may be unable to express this for quite a while. Finally, and maybe most importantly, I have become more convinced that the best precautionary measure I, as a client-centred therapist, can take, with respect to suicidal risks, is to remain the client's client-centred therapist and nothing else.

PATIENTS DIAGNOSED WITH OTHER KINDS OF PSYCHOSES

The diagnosis of schizophrenia

The preceding section described characteristics of therapy with psychotically depressed clients, those with depressive delusions. The clients who will be the main concern of this section are those whose psychotic condition is characterised by what psychiatrists diagnose as persecutory or megalomaniac delusions, hallucinations, and/or autistic withdrawal. Many of them will also be characterised by more or less incoherent speech, i.e. speech which the therapist will have great difficulty in following and understanding, or following it and understanding it will prove impossible for the therapist for shorter or longer periods of time.

These forms of psychotic ideation and behaviour are often associated with schizophrenia. However, I prefer to avoid using the terms 'schizophrenic' or 'schizophrenia' because this diagnosis, in my mind, is so controversial as to be rendered useless. Nobody knows whether schizophrenia is an independent disease entity or not, or whether the many different conditions diagnosed with a proliferation of sub-diagnoses under the heading of schizophrenia belong to the same disease entity or represent separate diseases — or whether it is a disease in the ordinary sense of the word, or not. Furthermore, hypotheses of aetiology vary widely, and the way the diagnosis is applied in psychiatry is very unreliable, i.e. different psychiatrists do not agree to a statistically very high degree among themselves on which patients are suffering from schizophrenia and which are not. The reliability of the use of the broader term 'psychosis' is much higher, meaning that it is much easier to reach agreement about the existence of psychotic features (predominantly delusions and hallucinations) in a patient's condition. Still, this has no practical consequences for the client-centred therapist. Mention of it is only done to explain why the term 'schizophrenia' is not encountered more often in this book, and especially in this section.

'Out of contact'

All psychotic patients, though, including psychotically depressed patients, have one thing in common: they are often experienced as being 'out of psychological contact'.

Psychotic patients do not, to quite the same degree as the ordinary client population of client-centred therapy, include the listener in their momentary experience, in the sense that they do not quite as extensively empathise with, and accommodate, the listener's need for the kind of information that enhances the likelihood that the listener will understand. John Shlien (1961) sees this as a crucial feature of psychosis. He writes (p. 296):

> The mind emerges through a process of communication. This involves social interaction on the basis of what Mead calls 'significant symbols' (usually words). A significant symbol is one that is 'reflexive,' i.e., when it is used it *presupposes another* person, anticipates his response, involves on the user's part some sense of how that other will feel ... *Acknowledging the other is essential to the existence of mind*, from beginning to end.

It is precisely a non-acknowledgement of the other (the therapist included), which seems, to me, to be the central feature of the experience of being 'out of contact' with psychotic clients. One has the impression that these clients do not, to the same degree as others, want to be understood.

This, of course, has important practical consequences for the client-centred therapist, because it touches on the very conditions for therapy to occur, particularly when empathic understanding is defined as understanding that which the client wants the therapist to understand, (see p. 123).

Rogers (1957, 1959) wrote two important papers in which he described his theory and approach to psychotherapy concisely and with careful definitions of the main concepts of the theory. In his 1957 statement (p. 96), Rogers listed the first condition of therapy as follows: 'Two persons are in psychological contact.' In the 1959 statement (p. 213) the same condition read: 'Two persons are in contact', and the following definition of contact was given (p. 207): 'Two persons are in psychological contact, or have the minimum essential of a relationship, when each makes a perceived or subceived difference in the experiential field of the other.' This last definition might cover even the relationship with a psychotic client who is experienced by the therapist as being 'out of contact'. In my opinion, this definition of contact is too broad to be one of the conditions for client-centred therapy to occur. It can, at most, be a pre-condition. This is because one of the other conditions of therapy says that the therapist must try to empathically understand the client, i.e. understand the client from the client's inner frame of reference. For this to happen, of course, the therapist must experience the inner frame of reference of the client or he must experience the client as wanting him, the therapist, to understand something, but this is exactly what the therapist does not always do with clients diagnosed with psychosis. Therefore he experiences the client as being 'out of contact' even if the two, therapist and client, make a 'perceived or subceived difference in the experiential field of the other'. In my mind, for normal client-centred therapy to occur, the contact between client and therapist must be such that the therapist experiences, at least to a minimal degree, the inner frame of reference of the client. This means that the client must seem to the therapist to have a wish to disclose some of his inner goings on to the therapist, and wish to have this disclosure understood by the therapist. What does the client-centred therapist do, then, when he does not experience such an inner frame of reference of a patient he wants to interact with, or such a wish of the patient, i.e. when he experiences the patient as being 'out of contact'? My preferred answer to that question is that he empathises with the patient on the very concrete level of the contact reflections of pre-therapy.

Pre-therapy

Pre-therapy was developed by Garry Prouty during the last three decades of the last century and is most fully laid out in his 1994 book. It is a truly person-centred approach, for use when persons are 'pre-expressive' as Garry Prouty has it, i.e. when the therapist experiences no inner frame of reference from which he can empathically understand the other person. The empathy of the therapist applying pre-therapy is to the other person's immediately observable behaviour and it is communicated by way of several types of 'contact reflections'. In the following section, I'll give a short survey of the contact reflections of pre-therapy and their rationale, because they'll be encountered intermittently in the examples, in this chapter and the following, of therapy with psychotic and near-psychotic clients. I hope this may stimulate readers to seek further acquaintance with pre-therapy, for example in the works of Garry Prouty (1994) and Dion Van Werde (1994a, 1994b). In my view, studying Garry Prouty's book, and having experience with pre-therapy, is a must for any client-centred therapist who considers working with the more withdrawn psychotic and near-psychotic clients in psychiatric contexts. Further, I am of the opinion that it should be a must in any training programme for client-centred therapy and counselling, because near-psychotic clients can be met in all kinds of settings, and these clients do often, rather subtly, move in and out of contact. It is important, therefore, that the therapist can follow them by moving fluently back and forth between 'normal' empathic understanding responses and the so-called 'contact reflections' of pre-therapy.

The client for whom client-centred therapy was originally developed has a rather solid sense of himself from which he expresses himself with the intention of being understood by the therapist. He is in contact with himself, with others, and with the world around him. This is what allows the therapist to have an experience of his inner frame of reference. However, it is exactly these 'contact functions' that seem impaired with many psychiatric patients, either continuously or more intermittently. These contact functions (with himself, with others, and with the world around him) are, in pre-therapy, called 'affective contact', 'communicative contact', and 'reality contact', respectively. Theoretically, the contact reflections attempt to restore and stabilise these contact functions.

Five distinct kinds of contact reflections are specified in pre-therapy, as follows.

1. *Situational reflections (SR)*

The therapist reflects the surrounding reality or milieu of the client, i.e. 'The sun is shining', 'People are talking outside', 'You are wearing a green jacket', 'We are both very quiet', 'The crows are making a lot of noise' etc.

Situational reflections tend to restore and facilitate the client's reality contact.

2. *Body reflections (BR)*

The therapist reflects the body posture or body movement of the client, either by imitating it bodily, or by verbal reflection of it, or both. For example: 'You look at the pictures on the wall-board', 'You have your head in your hands', 'You are gazing ahead of you', 'You look at me, I look at you', or, shaking his head: 'You shake your head, I shake my head'. Further, the therapist holds his hands to his ears as the client holds his hands to his ears, or the therapist paces the floor along with the client saying, 'We are pacing the floor'.

Body reflections tend to restore and facilitate the client's contact with his own body (realistic body image, reality contact).

3. *Facial reflections (FR)*

The therapist reflects his impression of the affective facial expression of the client, i.e. 'You look happy', 'You look worried', 'You look pleadingly at me', 'You look angrily at me', etc. Facial reflections tend to restore and facilitate the client's affective contact.

Often a facial reflection brings another emotional reaction to the face of the client and it is important to reflect this, too. If, for example, the therapist has reflected: 'You look angrily at me', and the client then looks scared, the therapist reflects: 'You look scared'.

4. *Word-for-word reflections (WWR)*

The therapist reflects, word-for-word, what the client has just said. With apparently incoherent clients, the therapist reflects the words and sentences or sentence-fragments he understands, or the words and sentences or sentence-fragments that seemed most meaningful to the client.

C: *It's all — the sexual thing is all there is — common and general.*
T: *The sexual thing is all there is, common and general.*
C: *They took me out; they give it to me to ameliorate me for it.*
T: *They give it to you to ameliorate you for it.*

Word-for-word reflections tend to restore and facilitate the client's communicative contact.

5. *Reiterative reflections (RR)*
The therapist repeats the reflections that have been most successful with respect to facilitating the contact functions and the experiencing process of the client. The excerpt above continues as follows:

C: *To prepare me.*
T: *To prepare you. (WWR)*
(Pause)
T: *You said: 'They give it to me to ameliorate me for it'. (RR)*
C: *They prepare me with the medicine, that's what it's for.*
(Later in the session, C tells with indignation of her conviction that her psychiatrist wants a sexual relationship with her and prepares her for it with the medication.)

I hope that the examples given above convey an impression of the extraordinary concreteness of contact reflections. Therapists who work with clients whose contact functions are firmly established are often unaware of the relatively high level of abstraction of their empathic understanding responses, because the client is expressing himself on the same level of abstraction. However, such is not the case with many psychotic and autistic patients. Their level of experience and expression is typically very concrete and the therapist must respond on the same level if there is to be any possibility of getting in touch with the patient. Very many attempts to contact these patients are way above their heads and therefore unsuccessful. Getting used to working at this very concrete level is not easy and it takes time. My own experience with pre-therapy is fairly short, and I am only now starting to feel comfortable with the concreteness of the contact reflections. When I first applied contact reflections, I felt almost condescending to the patient, or as if I were making a mockery of him, because my reflections were so totally literal. I helped myself to overcome this feeling by thinking of the relationship one has with an infant. Grown-ups spontaneously and lovingly reflect babies and small children literally. They say: 'My, aren't you crawling fast', or 'Oh, what a big smile', or 'You are painting it red all over', etc., and they look forward, lovingly, to the infant's 'next move'. As time has gone by, and as I have experienced the positive effects of my contact reflections in establishing contact with patients, I have come to experience the concreteness of these reflections as a gentle expression of my wish to get in contact with them. They express my acceptance of, and empathy with, the patient's behaviour, and my wish to continue to follow the patient. Most of my contact reflections hover softly somewhere between a declaration, which would have been a mockery, and a question, which would not only have been a mockery, but also an intrusion. For me, a very important aspect of contact reflections is that they have enabled me to be with patients who are very scared and fearful of contact, in a non-imposing, non-intruding, and non-demanding way. The contact reflections help me meet these patients where they are, in a way that, to me, feels truly person-centred.

It should be mentioned that pre-therapy can be applied with all 'out-of-contact' persons, not only psychotically withdrawn patients. Experiences have been made with persons who are not only psychotically withdrawn, but also intellectually retarded (Prouty, 1994); with persons who are withdrawn as a result of depression in combination with mental retardation (Prouty and Cronwall, 1990); with the street children in Brazil (Morato, 1991); and with persons in advanced stages of dementia, for example persons suffering from Alzheimer's disease (Van Werde and Morton, 1999). With respect to persons suffering from dementia, the aim with contact reflections is not, of course, the restoration of their contact functions to their former level, but the facilitation of their contact functions of the moment to the fullest possible extent.

Example: Having a nice time

This example is with a former very well functioning woman (C), who is now suffering from Alzheimer's disease. She is also a relative of mine. With such persons, contact reflections can be almost instantaneously effective in facilitating actualisation of their remaining potential for being in contact, and, in addition, they are often the most meaningful way of relating with these persons, which is why I have chosen to include this example.

C never initiates any contact and spends most of her time either in her room or in the nursing home's shared living room, sleeping or staring ahead of her. If approached with questions or comments that demand awareness of past experiences or future possibilities or anything but the most concrete awareness of the 'here-and-now', she becomes evidently uncomfortable and sometimes even fearful.

L finds her at the garden window, staring ahead of her as usual. L sits down besides her, turns towards her and takes her hand. L knows that C likes this physical contact.

L: *I hold your hand. (SR)*
C: *(Turns towards me and smiles at me.)*
L: *I hold your hand and you smile at me. (SR, BR)*
C: *(Smiles even more broadly.)*
L: *We are sitting next to each other and you look glad. (SR, FR)*
C: *I am. Do I look nice? (Saying this, she looks down on her dress and smoothes out some creases in it. This is a major step forward because she*

normally does not show any interest in her looks or in other aspects of her surroundings.)
L: *You ask: Do I look nice? (WWR), and you smooth the creases in your dress. (BR)*
C: *Yes, I like it when I'm nicely dressed.*
L: *Yes, you like to look nice. (L smiles at her, squeezes her hand a little, and they sit a while in silence.)*
....
C: *(Looks out of the window.)*
L: *You look out of the window — at the trees and the bushes and the little pond. (BR, SR)*
C: *And the bird.*
L: *You look at the bird on the stone next to the pond. (BR, SR)*
C: *Yes, look, it's bathing!*
L: *Yes.*
(L and C watch the bird bathing for a while.)
C: *Where are we?*
(L tells her, responding to this 'in contact' request for information from L's own frame and silently enjoying C's display of initiative and interest.)

Comments
1. It seems evident to me that this 'contact reflecting conversation' (which continued for a while longer until C seemed sleepy, L stayed silent, and C fell asleep) optimally facilitated actualisation of C's remaining potential to be in contact.

2. The contact reflections helped not only C, but also L, to have the closest and most satisfying relationship possible. I am convinced that not only those suffering from dementia, but also their caretakers and relatives, can profit from the application of contact reflections because, with this form of contact, the relationship with the demented person again feels close and meaningful. This is an important point about contact reflections: as with the ordinary empathic understanding response process of client-centred therapy, contact reflections help one to maintain an acceptant relationship with the other person, i.e. they maximally minimise the risk of conveying conditional regard. This is also the kind of contact close relatives and friends normally want with the demented person. Empathising is as much for the empathiser as for the recipient of empathy.

With chronically autistic and withdrawn, possibly also intellectually retarded, psychotic patients, it can take a long, long time before there appear signs that the patient's contact functions are enhanced. Further, all patients will not develop to such an extent that they can profit from ordinary client-centred therapy. However, they will normally become able to participate in a wider range of occupational and leisure activities, thereby enriching their quality of life. I have no personal experience with long-term work with chronically autistic and intellectually retarded, psychotic, patients, because in my country, Denmark, these persons only come into a psychiatric hospital in acute crisis situations. Normally, they are cared for in small sheltered living facilities and psychiatric nursing homes. I will therefore refer readers to Garry Prouty's book (1994) for fine examples of application of the five kinds of contact reflections with these people and to the work of Deleu and Van Werde (1998) and Marlis Pörtner (2000) for examples of pre-therapy applied in their daily living milieu.

The following example, from my own practice, is characteristic of the way I apply contact reflections with less chronically psychotic clients, whenever I, temporarily, do not experience an inner frame of reference of the clients, i.e. I have no idea whatsoever of what is going on within them, and they don't seem to want me to understand anything.

Example: Fluctuating between contact reflections and ordinary empathic understanding responses

In our first three sessions, Lillian, diagnosed with paranoid schizophrenia, talked rather freely of her conviction that her new neighbours are out to kill her. A consequence of this conviction was that she started living in her apartment as if she were not there, so as not to attract any attention towards her, especially from the neighbours. She stopped going out, and she stopped opening windows, turning on the light and the water, using radio and television, etc. Finally she mustered all her courage and phoned the police to whom she, in a whisper, told of her predicament. The police offered to come and take her to the hospital. She accepted this offer with relief, and she takes part in the various activities of her ward with great pleasure. She feels safe and comfortable in the hospital. In the fourth session Lillian's condition has changed: all energy seems drained out of her, she sits with her head bent down so I cannot see her face, and she does not start talking as she did on her own initiative in the former sessions. She sits like this for some minutes, and I have no idea what is going on in her.

T: *We sit in silence and you have bent your head down. (SR, BR)*
(L stays in the same position for a while. Then she raises her head a little and takes both her hands to her head, pulling her hair and using her hair as 'handles' to shake her head.)
T *(Mirroring her gesture): You shake your head with your hair. (BR)*
(L lets her hands sink into her lap and turns to look at me with what to me

seems like an expression of hopelessness in her face and eyes.)

T: You look hopeless. (FR)

L (Looking down again): Yes ... I don't know.

T: You said: 'Yes', and 'I don't know'. (WWR)

L: I don't know what to say — I'm so tired.

T: Too tired even to talk, is that how you feel? (Normal empathic understanding response.)

L: Yes ... yes.

(There is a long pause, where T stays silent, and L remains motionless, with her head bent down, as in the start of the session. Then the loud 'cock-a-doodle-doo!' of a nearby cock is heard and L raises her head and looks towards the window.)

T: You look up at the sound of the cock. (BR, SR)

L (Turns towards me and smiles at me, and I smile at her.)

T: You looked up at the sound of the cock and now we smile at each other, and you look glad. (RR, SR, FR)

L: We used to have lots of animals at home when I was a kid; cocks, too; sometimes they kept everybody awake (giggles).

T (smiling): Feels good and funny, recalling that, right? (Normal empathic understanding response.)

L: Yes (looking sad), I wish I could be there again.

T: You look sad when you think of how you miss being at home as a kid. (FR and normal empathic understanding response.)

L: Yes, I wish I had my family, I feel so lonely, and I don't know what to do, I'm scared of returning home.

T: 'If I had a family to return home to, I wouldn't feel so lonely and scared', is that it? (Normal empathic understanding response.)

L: Yes, K (her primary nurse) proposed the other day, that I try to go home to my apartment with her, one of these days, to see how it feels, I think they want me to go home soon.

T: You think they see you as being ready to go home soon, but you don't feel ready at all. You feel they hurry you a bit? (Normal empathic understanding response.)

L: Yes, but I think I should try to go home with K.

T: You feel you ought to give it a try? (Normal empathic understanding response.)

L: Yes, I really don't know what to do, how I shall manage at home. I'm not so scared of the neighbours any more, but still, maybe I'll do something that disturbs them, so they'll complain about me to the janitor and have me thrown out of the apartment, that's what I'm thinking about all the time.

T: You just worry so much that you won't do things right at home, that you'll somehow displease your neighbours? (Normal empathic understanding response.)

L: Maybe — they have two children so they are four and I'm alone, and their apartment is the same size as mine ...

T: Feels as if you haven't got the right to occupy that much space when they have so little?

L: I know I've got the right, of course, but still … I guess I feel somehow guilty about it …

but that's only … it's weighing me down, the thoughts, they keep turning and turning around in my head. (Bends her head down and away again, saying this.)

T (again feeling somewhat out of contact with L): You said 'It's weighing me down' and you bend your head. (WWR of the part of the client's statement that seemed most meaningful to her combined with BR.)

L (after a long pause, almost inaudible): I don't think I can go home with K – do you think she will be annoyed with me?

T: I don't know, I wish I could tell you for sure that she wouldn't be, 'cause I guess you are really afraid to displease her? (Answer to L's question and normal empathic understanding response.)

L: Yes, she has done a lot for me and she offers to escort me home, and then I can't even think of trying.

T: Like there'd be nothing you'd wish more than to feel able to accept her offer and feel helped by it, but instead you feel burdened by it, is it something like that? (Normal empathic understanding response.)

L: Yes, very, and I don't know how to tell her.

T: Mhm, hm … How shall I tell her?

L: Mhm. (Stays silent for quite a while, looking rather thoughtful.)

T: You look thoughtful. (FR)

L: Maybe if we postponed it a week or two, maybe that would be OK with K. After all, I haven't been in hospital very long, not nearly as long as many of the other patients.

From this point on, the therapist feels in contact with L for the rest of the session. In this session and in the following ones, which follow much the same pattern as above, L expresses much deeper feelings of worthlessness, loneliness and anxiety about managing on her own. The problems with the neighbours are just the last event in a long and hard struggle to live a life as close to what she considers as normal as possible. She is offered the possibility of going into a sheltered living facility, and after thinking it over, in sessions, and with her primary nurse, she decides to accept the offer. With this decision, she feels no further need for psychotherapy, and she terminates, satisfied to feel much more hopeful about her future. The latest news about her is that she thrives well and is a much-appreciated member of the living facility.

Comments

Apart from the examples of contact reflections, the above therapy excerpt and vignette is characteristic of client-centred therapy with hospitalised psychotic clients in several other ways:

1. It is not unusual that the movement of psychotic clients is towards greater dependence on others in the form of more protected ways of living. These clients have held a concept of self as being self-supportive and independent, which, in the course of therapy, turns out to be contrary to their more immediately experienced needs and wishes. Realising this is often a very painful process for the client, although this was only to a limited degree the case with Lillian, who felt the accommodation of her dependency wishes in the ward as a great relief and rather quickly and easily accepted her wish for protection on a more permanent basis. The theory of client-centred therapy puts great value on the concepts of freedom, autonomy, and independence, and it can therefore be difficult for the client-centred therapist, especially if he is inexperienced with psychiatric clients, to accept fully the client's apparent movement towards greater dependency rather than less. However, independence can be as incongruent a feature of a person's self-concept as any other, and full acceptance of dependency wishes, and the consequences of these wishes, can be a pre-condition for any further development towards true independence. I've had many clients like Lillian, who have terminated therapy feeling good about a decision to enter into a more sheltered way of living, although they started out in therapy with a goal of becoming better at living independently. This is an example of the frequent experience of therapists, that the clients' original goals with therapy are often expressions of what turns out to be incongruent aspects of the clients' self-concept, i.e. they are expressions of internalised conditions of worth.

2. During the time of the session with Lillian, transcribed above, I participated in staff meetings with, among others, Lillian's primary nurse K. In these meetings, Lillian's situation and condition were discussed and it was in such a meeting that K advanced her idea of taking Lillian on a home visit. Although I knew Lillian might feel somewhat upset by this idea, I did not intervene with this plan on behalf of Lillian, as I did not, in the session, intervene in support of K's idea of trying a home visit. With the ultimate goal of protecting my therapy process with Lillian, I avoided becoming Lillian's advocate with K or K's with Lillian (see point 6 in the section about the 'double life' of the client-centred therapist in the medical model setting, p. 38). Knowing K to be a somewhat action-oriented and efficient nurse, I could empathise with her wish to accelerate the process with Lillian in accordance with the medical model, where the doctors and nurses, rather than the patients, are considered responsible for the patients' processes. It is in situations like this —

and such situations are very frequent — that I feel very supported by the principle of complementarity. This principle allows me to fully respect the inner frame of reference of Lillian, when with her, and the medical model frame of reference of K, when with her, without identifying with either, and without feeling disloyal to either, although they may sometimes seem to be on conflicting courses.

3. To Lillian, K's proposal of a home visit represented a minor crisis. This is characteristic of psychiatric hospitalisations. The medical model treats patients by all kinds of interventions; it is not inclined to see treatment as a process, but rather sees it as a series of discrete events. It is action- and result-oriented; it must make things happen to and with the patients. This is inherent in the medical model and it is intensified by the normal scarcity of beds, which necessitates a rather quick turnover. The medical model cannot fully respect the tempo and pace of the patients. For many patients, therefore, hospitalisation implies all kinds of crisis situations, which will be a frequent theme in therapy sessions. Clients talk about their experiences and relations with staff members, about different treatment plans proposed to them and about the treatment activities they are currently engaged in. In addition, events like involuntary admittance and involuntary treatment are, of course, often extremely traumatic for clients and can be the focus of therapy for many sessions. There are periods when most of my clients are concerned about and in pain from their different kinds of experiences with psychiatry and I can then wonder if the whole of the psychiatric system after all does more harm than good.

4. In the therapy excerpt with Lillian, there is an instance where my empathic understanding response is in the first person singular mode ('If I had a family to return home to, I wouldn't feel so lonely and scared', is that it?). I respond as if literally identifying with the client and I often do this with psychotic and near-psychotic clients, who typically do not feel much trust in others; rather, they tend to feel quite distrustful, isolated, and scared in their relationships with others. In my experience, responding in the first person singular mode can help these clients feel more safe and less isolated, because it allows for a clearer 'we' relationship as opposed to the 'I-thou' relationship that is implied in the 'You feel (or think, etc.)' type of response, which psychotic and near-psychotic clients can sometimes feel as confrontational, threatening and alienating. Responding in the first person singular mode seems to promote these clients' trust that I'm fully with them, and it also seems to help them better perceive my empathic understanding of them and my unconditional

positive regard for them. In the same vein, I sometimes find myself using the client's first name in my responses to clients who will typically, though, be less self-expressive than Lillian. This is my reaction to an impression I sometimes have that these clients feel threatened by the sheer experience of themselves as the agent or source of their own experiences. Addressing them by their first name, i.e. 'John looks sad' or 'John hears a menacing voice', sometimes feels natural as a way of expressing acceptance of the client's difficulty with experiencing himself as an 'I', and as a way of being respectful of the degree of closeness with his experiences which is currently tolerable to the client. Likewise, I sometimes talk with clients, about them and their experiences, in the third person, as if we were literally talking about somebody else, referring to the client as 'he' or 'she'. Fundamentally, I think, this is no different from the situation with more self-expressive clients, where therapist and client sometimes talk about different, less well integrated, aspects of the client's self-concept in a somewhat distancing way ('part of me/you feels angry' or 'the helpless me/you', for example). Addressing a client by his first name, though, and talking with the client about the client in the third person, is certainly more comprehensive than speaking about parts of the client, encompassing, as it does, that central aspect of a person that is the experiencing 'I'.

5. In the above example it will be noted that many of my tentative empathic understanding responses to Lillian take the form of relatively explicit questions, i.e. I ask explicitly, in one way or the other, 'Am I understanding you correctly?' In therapy processes where the therapist cannot rely on a stable, solid, and continuous experience of the inner frame of reference of the client, it is my experience that it is sometimes helpful to be explicit with the intention of trying to understand empathically. One does this by formulating one's tentative understanding as a question verbally, and not only with one's tone of expression. There are several reasons for this: first, of course, the therapist will normally feel more insecure about his empathic understanding with these clients than with more self-expressive clients, so asking comes naturally. Second, asking explicitly underlines the therapist's wish to understand, and it helps structure the therapy process for the client. In effect, by asking explicitly, the therapist says repeatedly and clearly to the client: 'I am here to try to understand you, that's what this therapy is about, I can't read your mind, and I'm not an expert on you.' Many psychiatric clients do, to a greater extent than most people, feel dependent on others, and furthermore, they are often very accustomed to relationships with helpers who regard themselves as experts on them. Many of them will therefore tend to perceive a

more declaratively formulated response from the therapist as the truth about them, whether they feel understood or not, or they will keep their possible disagreement to themselves unless it is very evident that they are only too welcome to disagree. Third, many psychotic clients have a very fragile sense of themselves as separate beings. They can feel convinced that others do read their minds, and they can feel fused with others, or they can feel very scared of losing their sense of separateness. Asking explicitly underlines in the clearest possible way that the client and the therapist are two separate persons. There is a delicate balance to strike between the feeling of a 'we relationship', which first person singular responses tend to enhance, on the one hand, and respecting the separateness of client and therapist, on the other. I normally feel that I strike this balance right when I follow up on a first person singular response with an explicit question, as was the case in my response to Lillian: 'If I had a family to return home to, I wouldn't feel so lonely and scared', is that it?

6. Looking back at this therapy excerpt with the wisdom of hindsight, I feel dissatisfied with a couple of my responses. I want to make a brief note of them in order not to mislead readers into thinking that I regard this example as an example of 'ideal' therapy.

When L, looking sad, says: 'I wish I could be there again', and I respond with: 'You look sad when you think of how you miss being at home as a kid', I think L would have felt better understood and more closely followed if I had responded with: 'You feel sad', i.e. if all of my response had been an ordinary empathic understanding response. I think L did disclose a feeling of sadness in her statement and responding with a reflection of facial expression in that situation is, I think, a little distancing, because I do not enter into her frame of reference in that moment as fully as would be possible. On the other hand, this is also a good example of the difficulties inherent in fluctuating between contact reflections and ordinary empathic understanding responses. Sometimes I underestimate, and sometimes I overestimate, the client's current level of contact with herself, others, and the world.

The other response of mine I feel dissatisfied with is my response from my own frame when L turns to me for reassurance that K will not be annoyed with her. I wish I could have empathised with the need for reassurance from me that she expressed with her question, instead of answering it. I wish I had said something like: 'You just wish so much that I could reassure you that she won't be annoyed, because you are really afraid to displease her?' Responding like this would, I think, have kept the option to focus on her current wish for reassurance from me better open to her. By answering her

question, I think I subtly directed her away from this issue and in
the direction of the issue of daring to talk to K about her disinclination
to accept K's offer. This is a good example of the reason I am reluctant
to respond from my own frame with ordinary therapy clients like
Lillian.

The importance of being able to apply the literal empathic reflections of
pre-therapy with psychotic clients is also highlighted by the history of
research into client-centred therapy. As mentioned in the Introduction
(see p. 7), Rogers and his co-workers (1967) made a comprehensive
investigation of client-centred therapy with patients suffering from
schizophrenia (the Wisconsin project) in the first half of the 1960s. It
was the first time client-centred therapy was applied with this
population. Before that time, it had more or less exclusively been applied
with much more well-functioning and better-integrated 'neurotic'
clients. The results of the project were ambiguous and somewhat
disillusioning as to the effectiveness of client-centred therapy with
persons diagnosed with schizophrenia. Rogers (ed.) writes (1967, p. 80)
that 'In many respects the therapy group taken as a whole showed no
better evidence of positive outcome than did the matched and paired
control group'. Further, Rogers (ibid., p. 92) writes: 'our therapists —
competent and conscientious as they were — had over-optimistic and
in some cases seriously invalid perceptions of the relationships in which
they were involved'.

On the other hand, it was also documented that the clients who had
received the highest levels of the core conditions did better than those
who received the core conditions on lower levels (ibid., p. 91).

I think that a major reason for the outcome of the Wisconsin project
was that the therapists in the project did not to a sufficient degree
acknowledge how much the patients were 'out of contact', although
Rogers does write that relationship formation seems more important to
the schizophrenic client than self-exploration (ibid., pp. 75–6). At that
time pre-therapy had not yet been developed, so these therapists may
have tried to understand the clients empathically, from within the clients'
frames of reference, even when they did not experience an inner frame
of reference of the client, or a client wish to be understood. In such a
situation, there is a tendency for the therapist to try to 'guess' at the
inner frame of reference of the client, to make it up himself, so to speak.
This, of course, is not empathic understanding; it works more like a
subtle form of interpretation, but it can be the only alternative to
terminating therapy for the therapist who does not know about pre-
therapy. Such 'guessing' at the inner frame of reference of the 'out-of-
contact' client can be beneficial. It can just as well, though, lead to the
defences of the client becoming more rigid or, alternatively, crumbling,
with the inherent risk of further psychotic denial, distortion, and

withdrawal. Further, many of the therapy clients of the Wisconsin project felt apprehensive or downright antagonistic towards the offer of therapy. This is not uncommon with psychotic patients. If the therapist expects to do 'normal', regular therapy with such patients, he expects too much. In this case, there is the risk that the therapist's 'congruently expressing himself' is confused with a cathartic release of the therapist's frustration with the patient. (For a more detailed critical review of the Wisconsin Project, see Sommerbeck, 2002b). Before I became acquainted with pre-therapy, I often felt frustrated in my interactions with the more withdrawn patients, but with pre-therapy, I feel much more at ease with withdrawn patients and my relationships with them develop in a more uniformly positive way. This does not mean that the patients are 'cured', but it does mean that their level of functioning becomes better and they are less 'out of contact'. Alternatively stated: they become able to share a larger part of life with the rest of us. These impressions of mine, I think, are supported by the fact that, in contrast to the Wisconsin project, research into the effect of pre-therapy has shown more unequivocal beneficial results (Prouty, 1994).

In the German study mentioned in the introduction (see p. 7), Teusch (1990) found that the more disturbed the patients were in the beginning of the therapy, the more likely they were to fail to benefit from the therapy. They also found that standard procedures with regular sessions were not possible with the most disturbed patients. This seems to me to corroborate my contention that pre-therapy is a 'sine qua non' with the most disturbed patients of psychiatry: it is the only way to have a truly unconditionally acceptant relationship with them. It is also evident that, with these patients, the therapist must leave his office and meet the patient when and where the patient will be most responsive. Furthermore, I think it highlights the importance of psychiatric nurses being experienced with pre-therapy, because they are in an optimal position to apply it in their daily contacts with patients, whether in the psychiatric hospital or in the psychiatric nursing home. Readers interested in the application of pre-therapy as an integrated element in the 'milieu therapy' and daily care of the most disturbed patients of psychiatry are, again, referred to Dion Van Werde (1998), Deleu and Van Werde (1998) and Marlis Pörtner (2000).

My own most general impression of pre-therapy, as compared with ordinary client-centred therapy, is that the contact reflections of pre-therapy allow the therapist to be with the patient as unconditionally respectful and acceptant of the patient's own process, as do the tentative empathic understanding responses of ordinary client-centred therapy. Pre-therapy is, to me, a 'being beside' this other person, who seemingly does not wish to be understood; client-centred therapy is both a 'being beside', and understanding of, this other person, who clearly wishes to be understood. In the end, I think, both the very concrete empathic reflections of pre-therapy, as well as the more abstract empathic understanding responses of client-centred therapy, can be said to facilitate actualisation of the other person's most constructive potentials. It is of less importance whether this is the other person's contact capacities, as is often the case with pre-expressive persons, or the other person's capacity to deepen his level of experiencing, as is often the case with self-expressive persons.

OTHER CHARACTERISTICS OF THERAPY PROCESSES WITH PSYCHOTIC CLIENTS

Psychotic clients do not seem 'out of contact' all the time, in the sense that the therapist does not experience an inner frame of reference of the client, or a wish to be understood. The most autistic persons will seem 'out of contact' in this way almost all the time, but with the more floridly psychotic persons the problem is often not so much the absence of the experience of an inner frame of reference. Rather, the difficulty lies in following the client continuously in a world that can be extremely unrealistic, seen from the perspective of consensual reality, and where the client may jump incomprehensibly from one place to the other. It is important that the therapist has a great tolerance for his own 'not-understanding'. The therapist will understand in bits and pieces, but he must tolerate that he cannot see any connection between these bits and pieces. What the client says can seem very fragmented, and in following this the therapist's responses will be fragmented, too; one response feels dissociated from the preceding one and from the next to come. This can also happen with clients who are not psychotic, but not in any way near the regularity and frequency with which it happens with psychotic clients. Therapy with these clients is an exercise par excellence in 'holding and letting go'. It is important that the therapist does not hold on to the understanding of one moment in order to save his own sense of continuity, but lets go of this understanding in order to follow the client's next move, even if it seems contradictory to the one preceding it.

Particularly, clients diagnosed with megalomania and mania will often talk in a fast, seemingly endless, stream of associations, where they leave out many steps in their chain of reasoning. The therapist can experience these clients as being under a huge pressure to talk, as if the client, although self-expressive, talks for the sake of talking, alone, not because he wishes to be understood. If the therapist wants to do his job, of following and understanding empathically, with these clients, it can be necessary to interrupt the client's stream of talk quite forcefully with a cry of 'Wait a minute, let me see if I have understood you …' or something to the same effect. If the therapist does not do this, he will, in all likelihood, be left totally behind, and, in the process, come to feel ever more out of contact with the client. By insisting on doing his job of trying to understand, on the contrary, the therapist will experience an increase in his sense of mutuality in the contact with the client. He will also experience an increase in the client's interest in the contact, as if the client is slowly realising that the therapist truly wants to understand him, that the therapist is not out to correct him, silence him, or whatever. Interrupting fast streaming monologues of clients in this way helps structure the relationship for the client, and it facilitates the client's trust in the relationship, because the client is not left alone by the therapist giving up trying to follow the client. Barbara Brodley (1998, p. 25) characterises one (out of five) criterion for making tentative empathic understanding responses as follows: 'When the therapist feels an impulse or desire to express and communicate his or her self while immersed in the attempt to empathically understand'. Brodley further expands on this: 'This impulse or desire to express oneself, which is resolved through expression of understandings, probably originates in the interpersonal and interactional nature of the psychotherapeutic relation. Inherent in an interpersonal relation is an expectation of an exchange — a back and forth characteristic of the interaction. The deeply empathically engaged therapist, however, seldom will experience any specific content from his or her own frame of reference that could serve as a vehicle for self expression. Thus, when the interaction involves almost exclusive focus and attention on the client member of the dyad, the therapist may feel the desire to be responsive and expressive through the vehicle of tentative empathic understandings.' This is a very significant point with many 'megalomaniac' and 'manic' clients.

Relative to the ordinary client population of client-centred therapy, it also happens more frequently with psychotic clients that the therapist must put questions about facts to the client, in order to have any chance of understanding the client empathically. An example of this is given in Rogers' therapy with Elaine (p. 112, T7).

The points made above have very clearly to do with psychotic clients' seemingly diminished 'acknowledgement of the other', compared with the ordinary population of client-centred therapy.

The most frequent way, however, in which the therapist will experience the psychotic client's diminished 'acknowledgement of the other' is by this client's disregard for consensual reality and by the corresponding necessity to tolerate the suspension of his, the therapist's, own sense of reality. This is necessary in order to be able to fully enter the client's frame of reference, i.e. in order to get to know the client's delusional and/or hallucinated world as the client knows it. The therapist must put his own notions of consensual reality out of the way of the client. This, of course, is in accordance with the principles of client-centred therapy, and in a psychiatric setting the therapist can also rest assured that the client has already been told, not one, but many times, that this or that viewpoint, or experience of his, is not deemed realistic. Suspending his own sense of reality, though, does not always mean that the therapist does not share his own sense of reality with the person he interacts with, when this person turns to the therapist to know about it. This happens rather often, especially with patients who are hesitant about engaging fully in a therapeutic relationship. It can comfort the patient, and lessen his anxiety about the relationship, to know that the therapist does not think, for example, that he is ruined (the depressed patient), or persecuted by killers (the paranoid patient), although the patient will continue to hold these beliefs. Likewise, it can sometimes happen that a patient will want to use whole sessions to discuss with the therapist their divergent views of reality. For example, the patient and therapist can consider together the probability that the stranger who came to the client's door did not come to kill him but maybe to try to sell him something. Such discussions can stimulate a lot of creativity and imagination in both the therapist and the patient, and they are often full of humour. They usually signify that the patient's development has progressed sufficiently, that his sense of himself is solidifying, and that he more freely and voluntarily seeks the help of the therapist for psychotherapeutic purposes, i.e. the patient is starting to define himself as a client and he is starting to belong to the ordinary client population of client-centred therapy.

Often, it is the therapist, not the psychotic patient, who initiates psychotherapy, or, rather, person-centred interaction; or, alternatively, the patient is persuaded to see the therapist, and does so only half-heartedly. Depressed patients do not have the hopefulness and energy to ask for psychotherapy. The patients with 'delusions of persecution' will rather feel that the police, lawyers, the government, etc. should help him. The 'manic' patient will be happily elated without a single worry to talk about. The 'megalomaniac' patient will feel that it is the therapist, others, the whole world, who needs his help. The 'autistic' patient tends to withdraw from contact rather than seek it. Finally, involuntarily committed patients will normally not reach out for any kind of help that does not give hope of their imminent release. However, if approached, or met, in a way that matches the patient's condition, and with an offer of interest rather than therapy, most of these patients will appreciate the person-centred interaction with the therapist although they will only very rarely tell the therapist so; they will just not turn the therapist away or flee from him. With many patients, the therapist, or, more correctly, person-centred practitioner, must be prepared to initiate the contact for the first of many, many 'sessions'. He must also, as already mentioned, be prepared to do this at times and places that have the greatest probability of finding the patient responsive, which will often be in the late afternoon (it is characteristic of many psychotic patients that they make an almost total day/night reversal) and not in the therapist's office, but maybe in the hallway or sitting room of the patient's ward, in the garden of the ward, or in the patient's own room. In addition, most psychotic patients normally appreciate shorter and more frequent talks than the usual one or two 50-minute session per week characteristic of therapy proper. With many patients, it takes a long time before the process has progressed so far that the patient will come to the therapist's office on the basis of a regular, pre-arranged, more 'normal' (but probably still somewhat elastic) schedule. Some patients with whom the therapist interacts do not get to that point; instead they terminate the relationship, perhaps thanking the therapist for some nice talks, when they feel free to turn their backs on psychiatry and to leave the psychiatric landscape in which the therapist is, after all, an inhabitant.

When the therapist approaches a severely psychotic patient, he must be prepared for the possibility that this may develop into a life-long relationship, or at least a relationship that will last until the therapist retires. Some clients, but far from all, will continue to want help from the therapist with their struggle towards full 'normalcy' when the more intense and regular therapy relationship has terminated. Although they find themselves satisfied with their own gains from therapy, they will want the therapist as a sort of 'security net', for help in crisis situations, in order for them to get through these situations in constructive rather than destructive ways, i.e. by opening up to their experiences rather than denying and/or distorting them. This may entail pre-arranged sessions with very long intervals (which the clients sometimes cancel because they have better things to do − and the therapist should welcome this), or the client may just want to phone the therapist to arrange for a few sessions when he feels in crisis. It is important to accommodate these wishes from (formerly) psychotic clients. They signify a healthy dependence, because these clients do seem to continue to be more prone to develop psychotic distortions of experiences, when under stress, than most people. This is in accordance with the stress/ diathesis model of psychiatry mentioned in the start of the section about the psychiatric context. It seems that although psychotherapy with a very long time perspective can help psychotic clients in a profound way, it cannot 'remove' a biological/hereditary disposition to be more easily overwhelmed and overburdened in crisis situations with a concomitant risk of psychotic breakdown. In my experience, a continuous, open-ended therapy relationship, on a very elastic schedule, reduces the risk of psychotic breakdown and augments the chances that the client will learn from a crisis situation to a very considerable extent. Furthermore, such a relationship is no burden to the therapist at all, rather it is a joy; the therapist will be amazed at how little effort it takes of him in order for the client to feel that he has received what he wanted, when he needs 'emergency help'. In addition, it feels like a privilege to be allowed to follow another person's development so closely for such an extended period of time.

Most psychotic clients, though, do not continue this far and this long in psychotherapy. Some clients terminate therapy when they have become able to live in a nursing home and continue their development there (see the example of Lillian, p. 75). Some terminate when they have become able to live outside an institution, satisfyingly for themselves and with the protection of disability benefit and sheltered day-care centres. Some terminate for reasons extraneous to the therapy and some terminate only to turn back later, which they may do several times. In short, the arrangements that need to be made for therapy with these clients are much more unpredictable than with the clients seen by the client-centred therapist outside the psychiatric setting.

Another aspect of the long-time perspective of therapy with psychotic clients is that psychotherapy will normally not be considered the primary treatment modality for psychotic patients in the psychiatric hospital. Some specialised long-term psychotherapy wards and small hospitals do exist, and in Belgium, for example, there exist psychiatric wards where the main influence comes from client-centred therapy and pre-therapy. This, however, is the exception. Under ordinary conditions, the primary treatment will be medication, which will normally remove or diminish psychotic symptoms relatively quickly and make it possible to transfer the patient from a closed to an open ward or to dismiss him from hospital altogether to continue the treatment as a day-patient or outpatient. As already mentioned, in most psychiatric hospitals, there is a scarcity of beds, which necessitates a quick turnover. Because of this, patients are sometimes dismissed too quickly and re-admissions occur frequently.

In the midst of all this rather robust activity, the therapist quietly and steadfastly continues with the therapy. It may seem inconsequential at first, but later the therapy will often come to be the most important treatment modality for the client and medication will be administered in a way that is more specifically geared to support the client's personal development rather than to remove psychotic symptoms. It is important that the therapist does not share any agenda that the goal of treatment is the (quickest possible) removal of psychotic symptoms. Such a removal of symptoms is not an indication of better psychological adjustment in anything but a very superficial way and recurrence of a psychotic episode is not a sign of psychotherapeutic failure. Medication can bring a patient quickly out of hospital and to a certain extent it can prevent psychotic relapses. However, it is psychotherapy and/or living in a milieu dominated by the core conditions to a sufficiently high degree that very slowly facilitate the development of the patient so he can live a still more fulfilling and gratifying life, more and more independent of the psychiatric system.

As may be surmised from the above, patience, patience and still more patience is a must in psychotherapy with psychotic clients and so is a tolerance for lack of narcissistic gratification or gratification of one's need to feel helpful. With many clients, it can happen that for several sessions in a row there will be no sign of progress. Both client and therapist may have to look back over a span of many months to realise that progress has taken place, and the experience of the client deepening his level of self-exploration will be more rare with these clients than with non-psychotic clients. Furthermore, when the client does deepen his level of self-exploration it is often only to revert to his former more superficial level in the next moment. In addition, clients may not indicate in any way that the sessions with the therapist are helpful to them, at least not until the later phases of therapy or the 'steady state' crisis intervention phase. On the contrary, they may indicate that therapy is of no benefit to them, that other patients might need the help of the therapist more, etc. In combination with the fact that progress is slow to come about and that relapses with psychotic episodes may well occur in the first long phases of therapy, this absence of more evident indications of being helpful can be a strain on the therapist's self-confidence. If possible, therefore, it is a good idea if the therapist does not work exclusively with psychotic clients. With respect to this, it is fortunate that non-psychotic clients sometimes find their way into the psychiatric setting as outpatients, and it also sometimes happens, as it has already been described, that staff members, especially on closed wards, need a few 'crisis sessions', either individually or in a group, after traumatic episodes on the ward. Relatives of psychotic clients may also need crisis help. Tasks like these, with comparably quick positive results, will help keep up the therapist's self-confidence and morale in periods where his therapies with psychotic clients may occasion him to doubt his competence as a therapist.

Example: Relating with an involuntary patient

Karen is a 25-year-old law student at university. This is the fourth time she has been in the closed ward, involuntarily committed. I know about her from staff meetings. The minute she is out of hospital, she discontinues medication, and her parents soon find her withdrawing from contact with them again. She stays in her small flat all the time, does not go out, does not open the door, does not answer the telephone. They know she is occupying herself with writing. Among other things, she writes lots of e-mails to different political and legislative institutions, of which she demands that they take action to prevent the military intelligence from silencing her by using illegal means to prevent her great plans for reforming the world from being published. The central theme of her plan is a circular village that will be built in the Saharan desert. Here the most intelligent people from all over the world will work together under her leadership. This will bring them an unsurpassed purity and peace of mind and after a year they will go back to their native countries and suffuse some of their most important citizens with their benevolence, which will then spread like ripples in the water.

In their extreme worry, her parents contact her GP, who obtains the necessary legal authorisation to have her re-admitted involuntarily. This is a situation in which the medical system is obliged to use force if necessary, because Karen is judged to be in a rapidly deteriorating psychotic condition that can be reversed with treatment, and furthermore she is judged to be a danger to herself by having stopped eating. At the time she is re-admitted, she has lost much weight.

Her psychiatric diagnosis is schizophrenia, paranoid and megalomaniac type. From Karen's point of view, though, being fetched by the police and brought to hospital against her will is just one more proof of the interference of the military intelligence. She spends most of her time during the first weeks of her stay in hospital writing letters of complaint, not only about the military intelligence but also about the psychiatrists and nurses who keep her on the closed ward and treat her forcefully with injections of medicine. She is convinced they are conspiring with the military intelligence.

I have read some of Karen's letters of complaint and although there are long passages that to me seem incoherent, there is also much dignity and a wish to make this world a better place to live in, which I find attractive. I feel like talking with her and trying to get to know her. Karen, though, is a patient who'd probably decline any offer of psychotherapeutic help. She does not feel herself to be in need of help; on the contrary, from her point of view, it is the rest of us who are in need of her help. Therefore, my own interest in her is the only reason I have to approach her.

I have passed her often, in the long hallway of the ward, nodding to her and saying 'hello', but she has looked right through me, with what seemed a condescending air, as if too busy with more important things to respond to me.

One day, though, I turn more directly to her, and the following dialogue develops.

T (therapist): I'd like to talk with you for a minute, if that's OK with you?
K (Karen, in a rather royal manner): It might be. (Apparently a little curious): What would you like to talk with me about?
T: I have heard about you in the staff meetings, and I have wondered about you, what you think of all this, being here and everybody thinking you are psychotic — I'd like to know your own thoughts about it?
K: I'm a person of jurisdiction, it will be taken care of, and I'm a person of jurisdiction.
T: You are a person of jurisdiction; it will be taken care of.
K: I'm a person of jurisdiction.
T: You are a person of jurisdiction.
K: There is a high court, the parents, and the doctors, there is a high court, and I'm a person of jurisdiction.
T: There is a high court, and you are a person of jurisdiction.
K: Yes, the parents and the doctors will learn their lesson.
T: You are a person of jurisdiction, so the high court will set things right, parents and doctors can't keep you here?

K: I'm wanted, they'll see to it.

T: Your affairs are so important that parents and doctors can't prevent justice from being done?

K: That's right, they are a case for the police, the parents can't cling to their children.

T: Parents should let go of their children, be able to do without them?

K: Yes, my sisters … (interrupts herself, resuming an air of condescending importance): Well, this will all be seen to; I'm a person of jurisdiction, I can't talk with you any more.

T (while Karen is already walking away): Thanks for letting me talk with you.

This dialogue took place in the hallway. I felt like I'd met the queen in the street and been allowed a few words with her. Afterwards I found myself pondering the question: what did Karen mean by talking about herself as a person of jurisdiction? Therefore, two days later, passing Karen in the hallway, as I was leaving the ward after a regular staff meeting, I turned to her again.

T: Karen, may I have a few words with you again? There was something you said, last time we talked, that I didn't understand?

K (with dignity): Please ask your question.

T: I have been wondering what you meant by saying that you are a person of jurisdiction?

K: There are laws about this, above the military intelligence; this case may very well be taken over by international authorities.

T: Do you mean that the laws hold for you, too? That military intelligence can't do whatever they want, so sooner or later you'll have a just trial and be known for what you are and get out of here?

K: Oh, they already know, I have notified them, and it is not only a question of getting.out of here; doctors and parents are a case for the police, and the military agency, too; (angrily) they want me to take medicine, but there are laws, the father is sick, he should be taken care of.

T: You are angry about the medication, because you feel it is the father who needs the medicine, not you?

K: The father infantilises the children, not me, but my sisters, they just go home all the time, but I try to protect them.

T: You want your sisters to have their freedom, too?

K: Yes, my father really clings to them; he is the child.

After a short interlude with talk about her family, Karen reverts to some final remarks about legislative authorities, and then she dismisses me like she did after our first talk.

I have three or four additional talks with Karen, much like the previous ones. After the twice-weekly staff meeting in the ward, I turn to Karen in the hallway with some question and she talks with both anger and dignity about the illegal interference of, variously, the military intelligence, the psychiatric system, and the parents, in her life. I notice that she allows me more and more time to talk with her before she dismisses me. I also notice that I have started to feel slightly uncomfortable that our talks take place standing up in the hallway with people passing by all the time.

When I arrive in the ward for the next staff meeting, Karen is there, seemingly expecting me, and for the first time she is the one who turns to me.

K: Do you have questions to see me about today?
T: Yes, as a matter of fact, I have. I had thought that I might talk with you after the staff meeting.
K: You are welcome.
T: I wonder if I could meet you in the small room, next to the television room; it is quieter there and we can sit down?
K: I'll rather wait for you in my own room.
T: I'll be there, then, at 10.30.

This becomes a routine for a while. Karen is in the hallway each time I arrive in the ward for the regular staff meetings. She asks me if I have something I wish to ask her about, and we agree to talk in her room. I secure time for these talks in my daily schedule, although they are not explicitly agreed upon with Karen.

Our talks still start with a question from me about something from our previous talk, which I have been thinking about. Karen courteously answers my question, and from there I respond with empathic understanding (or sometimes contact reflections, when I have no idea what is going on in Karen) to the best of my ability.

Karen is treated involuntarily with medicine and she now focuses more of her anger on the psychiatric system than on parents and the military intelligence. She seems more coherent now, and has started to see parents as victims of the system, like herself, rather than conspiring with the system. She expresses worry about her parents' marriage; she feels that her parents bind each other, and their children, in ways that are harmful to everybody.

All this is expressed in normal client-centred dialogue, and so is Karen's continued conviction that things will be taken care of by higher authorities, who recognise the importance of her plans for a worldwide reform. She feels well understood when I respond to this by saying that she feels no need for help from the psychiatric system, including me:

K: That's right: I like talking with you, it's a nice way of passing the time,

but I think the other patients need it more, because they are sick; it could help them think more clearly. You are a psychologist, so you don't know about medicine and diagnoses; one can talk more normally with you.
T: *It's not that you need it, but still it is nice talking normally with someone.*
K: *Exactly, I appreciate our talks in that way.*

At this point in our relationship, Karen is no longer judged to be in a condition that can legally justify involuntary detainment in a closed ward or involuntary treatment. She still holds the same psychotic convictions, but they don't take up so much space in her consciousness any more, and they don't prevent her from having rather normal, albeit somewhat formal, contacts with nurses on the ward. Her contact with her parents has also become better, and she eats normally.

When she is informed that she is no longer involuntarily committed, she chooses to go home at once. She declines any offer of outpatient treatment, including an offer of continuing her talks with me, and we all expect her to be back in hospital, involuntarily committed again, within half a year, because she will discontinue her medication.

This is exactly what happens.

I approach Karen like I did the first time, and the process described above starts all over again, but discrete changes in our relationship are noticeable. It doesn't last long before Karen expects me to come to see her after each staff meeting, and after a few talks, I am the one who has to finish because my time limit of about 50 minutes is reached. Karen accepts this gracefully. Karen doesn't relate to me as to a subordinate quite as extensively as she did the first time and she rather quickly tells me that she enjoys our talks, but still as a nice way of passing the time, not because she needs them. This means, however, that Karen is now the one who initiates our talks: she is waiting for me, eager to start, when I come to her room. The situation, where I am courteously allowed to ask her questions, belongs to the past.

The content of our talks is not much different from the first time, but shortly before she is released from hospital this time, she decides to take up her university studies again, where she left them three or four years previously. She is about to write her final thesis on the relationship between legislation and political reforms. She expresses the fact that she regards finishing her university education as a formality, and as a way to pass the time until she will be busy realising her worldwide reform plans, when the relevant authorities give her the signal to start.

A couple of months after her release, I am asked by a relatively new psychiatrist in the ward to contact Karen. He has had a call from her parents, who express worry about Karen's condition, and they feel I might have a chance to persuade Karen to start taking anti-psychotic medicine again. Apparently, Karen has told them that she appreciates her talks with me, and both the psychiatrist and her parents think it might be a good idea if I used Karen's trust in me as leverage towards making her accept medication. I refuse to accommodate this wish, explaining to the psychiatrist that it is of primary importance in my relationship with Karen — and probably a main reason for her trust in me — that I have no agenda on her behalf in my talks with her, that in our relationship she is the one who is the best expert on herself. I offer, though, that he can pass on the message that Karen is welcome to call me for an appointment if she might want to talk with me. The psychiatrist accepts this, although he evidently does not fully understand my position. Karen does not contact me.

Two or three months later, Karen is involuntarily re-admitted, in more or less the same condition as the previous times.

This time, however, she quickly asks to see me and she also seems to enjoy her contact with the nurses. The nurses, for their part, feel more comfortable with her, because they now have the impression that she becomes a little better each time she is re-admitted. They have started to see their work with her as meaningful, as opposed to her first admittances to the ward, which they felt to be a waste of time because there was absolutely no change in the process with her. During her first stays, they felt hopeless about her because she discontinued medication as soon as she got a chance to do so, and they regarded medication as the only necessary treatment modality for her. Now, however, she seems to take a little step forward by each admission, and especially her primary nurses put a higher priority on the quality of their contact with her, realising that this contact is also part of the treatment.

Towards the end of this stay, she tells me that she finds our talks useful for her. She feels relieved by having a chance to express all her thoughts and she also feels a calming and soothing effect from our talks, which she appreciates. She therefore asks for regular, pre-arranged, weekly sessions, so she can fit them into the rest of her weekly schedule in the ward. The content of our talks is still mostly about her grand scheme and the authorities that will take care of things, but she also tells me a little more detail about her family, and 'the parents' have become 'my parents'.

Furthermore, there are fleeting instances of disclosure of problematic experiences. She tells me that at home, when alone in her flat, she can sometimes feel as if she is surrounded by a sphere of glass, but when she is in the ward, she feels more real; she likes the contact with most of the nurses, and actually, she finds her stay in the ward rather agreeable. Particularly, she likes the meals very much; she just feels vehemently opposed to the medication. A few times she expresses doubt about her condition. Maybe the doctors have been right, maybe the feeling of being confined in a glass sphere has been a symptom of psychosis, but that is all over now, she is completely well again, this time she will surely finish her studies. This has evidently become more important to her: she now says that a university education, and after that a job, might promote her grand reform plans.

Towards the end of this stay, she starts referring to our talks as 'psychotherapy', and she considers the possibility of continuing them as an outpatient. Finally, though, she decides against this option, and at the end of our last talk in the ward, she thanks me for my help, convinced that we will never see each other again.

We do continue, however, next time she is involuntarily admitted, although the term 'involuntary' is now a little off the mark. When, as on previous occasions, her parents ask her GP to visit her, because they find her floridly psychotic and losing weight again, she immediately invites him inside and tells him that it will be OK for her to be admitted, but only if it is done involuntarily. Therefore, on her request, he fills in all the necessary papers and takes all the necessary steps for an involuntary admittance, whereupon her parents accompany her to the ward in all amicability. Here she is warmly welcomed and greets everybody nicely. She also asks to resume regular talks with me as soon as possible.

During her stay, this time, I leave for three weeks for a summer vacation. Upon my return, she is eagerly awaiting our next session:

K: I have so much to tell you about, I have really done a lot of thinking while you've been away.

T: You are almost bursting with all the things you've found out?

K: Yes, listen: we've been talking together so many times now, and I've been going over all that we have talked about. Things have become much more clear to me. I do think I have been psychotic each time I have been admitted and I've found out that writing my thesis has something to do with it. When I sit at home, writing, I get carried away with it, I get a feeling that my thesis will put everything right, that it must be written so it can do that, and I must also find ways to have it put into practice, to have my plan disseminated and put into practice. I have been thinking, while you've been away, that I overvalue the importance of it, after all it is only a thesis; it's not that all-important; the point of it is to finish my education, not to save the world, and it's a relief to realise that.

T: This insight you've come to feels very profound and like a huge relief and ...

K (interrupting): Oh, there is more. I also think that becoming psychotic

was necessary for me. I was too immature when I started at university; becoming psychotic, and coming here, and our talks have helped me see things more realistically, don't you think it can be seen like that?
T: *I suppose so, and this way of seeing it really feels true …*
K *(eagerly continuing): So I don't think I'm really sick, not schizophrenic or anything like that. It's more like a stress thing, the stress of writing the thesis, so I have agreed to take medication until I have finished my thesis. I think the medication will help me not to be carried away again. Now I just want to have my education over and done with and find a regular job.*
T: *So you see yourself as vulnerable to the stress of writing your thesis, and medication could be helpful with that? And with that you have some kind of feeling of starting afresh, is that it?*
K *(laughing happily): Yes, I'm quite excited about it.*

In our next few sessions before her release, Karen continues to discuss her new insights and her plans for her future in more detail. In the last session, she again considers the possibility of continuing her sessions with me as an outpatient. However, she comes to the conclusion that the decisions she has made have probably solved her problems, so she won't need outpatient psychotherapy. She makes sure, though, that she can call me for an appointment when she wants to.

Just before we say good-bye, she tells me that, although she doesn't expect to see me again, she doesn't feel 100% sure. All the other times, she has felt convinced that there would be no further admittances; this time she finds it unlikely but 'only time can show, so maybe we'll talk again'. She thanks me for my help and says: 'I feel our talks have helped me most, when I have been most psychotic — they sort of soften me up'.

This is the point to which our relationship has progressed thus far. I don't know if I will see Karen again.

Comments

This example contains many of the characteristics of what I call person-centred interaction with involuntarily admitted, so-called paranoid/megalomaniac patients, those who define themselves as prisoners of psychiatry. I'll make a short summary of them.

1. Many involuntarily admitted patients become 'swing-door' patients like Karen, because their views of themselves and their wishes are diametrically opposed to those of the psychiatric system. They therefore discontinue medication and contact with the psychiatric system when their condition has become so good that there is no legal authorisation to detain and treat them against their will.

2. The effect of medication is to suppress psychotic ideation; it doesn't remove (the potential for) psychotic ideation. Parallel with medication, psychotic patients need facilitation of psychological growth in order that they may search and find alternatives to a 'psychotic way of living'.

3. The non-directive person-centred way of interaction is eminently suited for involuntarily admitted and treated patients because the therapist does not in any way try to be helpful to the patient, or interfere with the patient; he solely wants to understand the patient. For most involuntary patients, the non-directive client-centred therapist is the first person with whom they have had the experience of feeling unconditionally accepted in a very long time.

4. Forceful interventions and efforts to persuade these patients to receive help and to change their conceptions of reality tend to be integrated into the delusional systems of the patients. Karen experienced the psychiatrists, in particular, as conspiring with the military intelligence agencies. This is one reason, I think, that it can be legitimately asked if the obligation and right given to psychiatry, to interfere forcefully in certain, specified, situations, with persons like Karen, does not do more harm than good. Sometimes, at least, it seems to me that it, basically, stimulates these persons towards more, rather than less, unconventional thinking and perception of reality, although medication, when taken by the patient, may mask this development.

5. In the beginning, motivation for interaction with the patient is supplied by the therapist. The patient expresses no wish for help. This, though, does not necessarily mean that he will not appreciate being understood, but it is very clearly the therapist's own wish to come to know and understand the patient that fuels the process for a sometimes very long beginning.

6. With patients like Karen, it becomes evident that attitudinal accommodation to the patient is necessary: the therapist behaves complementary to the attitudes of the patient in order to remain fundamentally non-directive and maximally minimise the risk of conveying conditional regard. In the case of Karen, I behaved a little like a subordinate to royalty. Of course, the therapist cannot and should not exceed his personal limits to this end. It is my experience, though, that most psychotic patients are very sensitive to the personal limits of the therapist. As long as the therapist is not experienced as disrespectful, or as a threat, the personal limits of the therapist will rarely be challenged.

7. In the same vein, it is noteworthy that Karen carefully avoids engaging me in discussions about her diagnosis and medication. It has been my experience that psychotic patients often, but by no means always, reserve such discussions for their psychiatrist; they seem to want to protect their relationship with the psychotherapist from this sensitive topic until they feel better prepared to deal with the issue. Of course, I react complementarily and non-directively to this, by not raising the issue. From my experience with Karen, during our last sessions, I suspect she may soon raise this issue with me — i.e. if she returns to resume our relationship.

8. A beautiful instance of complementary accommodation is supplied by Karen's GP when he admits her involuntarily on her request. Relationships with psychotic people are replete with such paradoxical phenomena. It is important that they are not questioned nor confronted, as they normally represent a constructive, albeit ambivalent, transition from avoidance to attraction with respect to treatment, and with respect to contact with others.

9. I still do not understand the meaning of Karen's repeated reference to being a 'person of jurisdiction' and there is a lot more she has talked about in sessions, especially the first ones during her hospital stays, when she was most floridly psychotic, which I do not understand. This is an example of the necessity of tolerating what seems incomprehensible, illogical, and incoherent, of feeling comfortable with not-understanding, and of letting go of a topic when the client moves to the next, whether you have understood anything or not. Perhaps some day Karen will make me understand what it means to her to be a 'person of jurisdiction'; perhaps I shall never understand.

10. The process with Karen has also been characteristed by its irregularity, by its length (I have known Karen for about two years by now), and by the changes that have taken place: still shorter hospital stays, a diminution of angry and hostile feelings, a richer repertoire of mutuality in her relations with others, and easier access to self-expression.

11. The example also shows the short-term perspective of medication as opposed to the long-term perspective of a therapeutic relationship. Furthermore, if Karen returns to resume her contact with me, she may soon wish this relationship for its therapeutic rather than purely social aspects, thereby developing it into a primary treatment modality for her.

12. In some of the sessions with Karen, when she was most psychotic, I felt I had lost contact with her inner frame of reference. In these instances, I applied verbal, pre-therapeutic contact reflections (Prouty, 1994), which quickly re-established contact with her inner frame of reference. A few examples of this are given in the very first excerpt of dialogue with Karen, when I reflect some of her utterances word for word, because I have no idea what it is she wants me to understand, if anything at all.

13. The necessity of protecting the non-directive relationship, when asked to take on the role of a directive expert, is exemplified by my refusal to accommodate wishes, from Karen's parents and psychiatrist, that I contact Karen on behalf of the medical model to try to persuade her to resume her medication. Evidently, the therapist's manager, probably the patient's chief psychiatrist, has to have some understanding of, and respect for, the role of this relationship in the total treatment of the patient for this to be possible. On his side, though, the therapist also has to acknowledge and accept his dependency on the patient's chief psychiatrist for having the opportunity to relate with an involuntary patient at all. It is the psychiatrist's application of the laws of use of force in psychiatry which makes the relationship possible. This is particularly clear with a patient like Karen, who terminates her relationship with me, as with all other representatives of psychiatry, as soon as her psychiatrist releases her. To me, as I think it would to any client-centred therapist, this poses an ethical dilemma which I have not been able to resolve: am I, after all, participating in forcefully intruding upon the patient, and restricting the freedom of the patient, when I engage in a person-centred relationship with the patient in a context of coercion? Is the progress, as judged by others, and to a somewhat lesser extent and in a different way by herself, of a patient like Karen, relevant for this question, at all? Does the end justify the means? Do I, in the end, do more harm than good by associating myself with a psychiatric prisoner like Karen? Am I tacitly condoning, with one hand, what I oppose with the other? Should I, rather, make an effort to have somebody pay me, and others, to go out and try to establish person-centred relationships with these people where they are, when they are not within the realm of the law of use of force in psychiatry? The line of questions pertaining to this ethical dilemma seems endless.

14. The almost total lack of narcissistic gratification for the therapist is exemplified by the fact that it is only in our most recent contacts that Karen tells me that our talks are helpful to her, and then only in a rather limited way. Patients like Karen will more likely express

their feeling of not needing the therapist's help, but they'll continue to see the therapist for other reasons, for example as a nice way of passing the time, as was the case with Karen.

15. The slowness of the process is evident from the fact that the process with Karen, as described, spans about two years. The signs of progress are very far between; for long periods of time, nothing seems to happen, and the talks can feel very repetitive. Had it not been for the fact that Karen developed a wish for our talks, whether as a nice way of passing the time or for any other reason, my interest in our relationship would probably have waned.

16. The necessity for the therapist of shuffling between two very divergent conceptualisations of reality should also be evident in this example. The principle of complementarity allows me to be with Karen in her private reality during our talks, and with the medical model's consensual reality, where Karen's reality is considered delusional, between our talks, without feeling that I compromise either reality. The illustration, however, also contains an example where I do not succeed in this, i.e. an example of what I, with an expression borrowed from Marvin Frankel (personal communication, 2002), would call 'therapist bias within an empathic context'. In one of our talks Karen says: 'I like talking with you, it's a nice way of passing the time, but I think the other patients need it more, because they are sick; it could help them think more clearly. You are a psychologist, so you don't know about medicine and diagnoses; one can talk more normally with you'. I respond with: 'It's not that you need it, but still it is nice talking normally with someone'. This is a very partial empathic reflection; it totally misses empathy for Karen's altruism and her concern for the other patients. The reason for this lack of empathy was a sudden identification of mine with the medical model. Thoughts about 'megalomania' and 'lack of insight into her own condition' flashed momentarily through my mind, i.e. I turned 'diagnostic' and I put my 'medical model perspective' in her way, with the consequence that my unconditional positive regard for her diminished and I could not be empathic. Shuffling between the two divergent realities of patients and the medical model is easier said than done, when the therapist, outside of sessions, is all the time exposed to the medical model way of thinking, and I do not always succeed.

Example: From pre-expressive and reluctant to self-expressive and highly motivated

In the following, I'll tell the story of a more complete and continuous process with a psychotic patient by painting with a broad brush rather than delving into the details of concrete dialogue.

When he was 23, Joel was involuntarily admitted to the closed ward of the regional psychiatric hospital in a floridly paranoid condition, convinced of the existence of a conspiracy towards him with the ultimate aim of killing him. He lived with his parents, and the immediate occasion for his admittance was an assault on a business associate of his father, who had been invited to dine with the family. Joel became convinced that this man was one of the conspirators, and the one who had been appointed to kill him. To protect himself, he suddenly launched out at this man with a knife, but was prevented from doing any serious harm by both the man and his parents.

At this point in time, his parents' worries about him had been growing steadily for a couple of years because Joel had lived still more secretively and isolated with them, and their contact with him, too, had deteriorated badly. They had tried to reason with him, to leave him in peace, to persuade him to participate in various activities with others — anything they could think of to get him out of this condition, but all in vain. They had, of course, also done their best to have him see a psychiatrist. Still, they had refrained from using, or asking others to use, forceful means. As a consequence of Joel's demonstration of violence, though, they called their GP, who initiated the necessary legal procedures to have Joel compulsively admitted to the closed ward of the psychiatric hospital.

This forceful admittance was as traumatic for Joel as it was for his parents. His parents ached with all kinds of painful feelings at having occasioned forceful means being used toward their son, and Joel was convinced that the hour of his being killed had arrived, without him being able to do anything to prevent it. He was awfully scared, and the medical treatment he was submitted to, against his will, made him even more scared, because he was convinced that he was being slowly poisoned. He would only eat and drink what his parents brought him, and he would talk to nobody but them. It was mostly through his parents that staff learned a little about Joel's experiences. It was also to his parents that he incessantly expressed his wish of going home.

In their desperate efforts to secure anything that might entail the slightest hope of being helpful to their son, his parents expressed their wish that Joel might be offered psychotherapy, and this was the occasion for my initiating contact with him.

Not that there was much contact to speak of. This was before I became acquainted with the contact reflections of pre-therapy, so I mostly stayed silent, too, or I made some 'empathic guesses', or I commented on what I found appropriate from what went on in me, including my wish to talk with him and my feeling of helplessness about how to get into contact with him. I had the impression that nothing of this was helpful to him. During our meetings, he was mostly lying on his bed with his back turned towards me, or sitting in a chair listening to rock music, which I then listened to with him, and sometimes commented a little upon. Listening to the music which he listened to was the way of being with him that felt most comfortable to me in the start of our relationship. I am unsure, though, that Joel reciprocated my sense of sharing in this listening, in the ordinary sense of the word 'share'. He has never commented upon it. When I asked him if he would rather be left alone, he invariably answered 'yes', and I left him. Normally, I asked him this question after about 10 or 15 minutes, mostly, in all truthfulness, to get out of the situation myself, because, basically, I felt very unwelcome and found this exceedingly uncomfortable. It was only the fact that he did not actively ask me to leave, and his parents' deep hope and conviction that psychotherapy would help in the end, which made me continue.

Little by little, though, his condition became better, at least from a psychiatric point of view. With staff members of the ward, he started to answer questions about, and comment upon, the daily, concrete, realities of the ward; he started to participate, with other patients, in the ordinary meals of the ward; and on outings with his primary nurse, he could talk a little with her about the weather, what they passed by, etc. The one thing he never spoke about, though, was himself, and when asked how he felt, he invariably answered 'fine'. In addition, he started to accept medication as part of the daily routine. Everybody had the impression that he had become better at conforming to consensual reality, but also that it was a very superficial improvement. Still, it was the kind of improvement that would make further detainment in a closed ward illegal, and, with the approval of his parents, who also found him better, he returned home after having stayed in the ward close to three months.

In my 'sessions' with him, though, there was not much change. The only change seemed to be that I rarely found him in bed any more. Now I mostly found him in his chair, listening to music, which I then listened to for a while, too, before I left him again.

At the time of his returning home, his parents asked for regular appointments with me, on his behalf, which I accommodated with a half-hour session a week. This marked a change in our relationship, because he took the initiative to say that he didn't find the sessions of any use to him: he only came to accommodate his parents' wish. I responded to this with empathic understanding upon which he decided to leave after about 10 to 15 minutes.

For several months, then, I scheduled weekly, half-hour sessions with him, of which he rarely used more than 15 minutes, most of these in silence. He mostly sat staring down at the floor, with his head turned slightly away from me, so I couldn't see his eyes. I felt very much 'out of contact' with him and quite discouraged about the relationship: nothing seemed to happen. Still, this was the only offer from psychiatry, apart from consultations with a psychiatrist concerning medication, which he did not flatly refuse to accept. (He had been offered sheltered occupation, sheltered living facilities, attending a day-care centre, etc.)

Then our relationship changed rather abruptly. One day Joel brought a big bag to the session and took out a pile of books, which he stacked on the small table next to his chair. He told me he had done quite a lot of reading lately, which he wanted to discuss with me. It turned out that he had marked a lot of sections in the books quite systematically, and he wanted me to read the marked sections and tell him what I thought about them. This was the first time in our relationship I felt he truly wanted something for himself from it. He might not want psychotherapy, but he evidently wanted my comments on some of the stuff he was reading. I accommodated his request and for quite a while we developed a routine where I spent most of the time reading and commenting and Joel asked questions, evidently interested, with respect to the section I had read and my comments on it. He did not comment much himself, though, and my tentative empathic understanding responses mostly resulted in his falling silent again and withdrawing a little from the contact. At this time, our relationship seemed more 'therapist-centred' than 'Joel-centred', because I was expressing myself much more than he was, and I wondered if it would ever evolve into an ordinary client-centred therapy relationship, or what would come of it. Still, Joel now obviously wanted our sessions for his own sake, and the schedule was changed to 45 minutes a week to have time enough for Joel's 'literary' agenda.

First, Joel brought popular books on philosophy and psychology, and some mutuality in the contact developed from my efforts to understand Joel's questions well enough to feel able to formulate a response to them. I was worried about the risk of placing myself in the role of 'expert', and I was therefore very explicit that my comments were my comments only, not facts, and that others would comment differently, and I often accompanied my comments with what I thought others might have commented. I also asked

Joel about his reactions to my comments, but mostly he answered: 'I don't know'. He still seemed to withdraw from my interest in his experience, as if he felt this interest as an intrusion.

Later, Joel brought popular books on psychiatry and asked all kinds of questions, particularly about schizophrenia. This developed, very tentatively, into Joel's sharing a little about his own experiences and asking me more specifically to comment on these. The dominant questions were: Did I think his conviction, that somebody wished to kill him, was a delusion? Did I think medication was necessary? To these questions, I responded with what amounted to an invitation to psychotherapy. I told him that I could surely understand that these questions, and finding answers to them, were of vital importance to him, and that I'd be very interested to hear all his thoughts about these issues and try to understand them, hoping that in this way we might find answers to his questions. At the same time I expressed my opinion that I found it most likely that his conviction that somebody wanted to kill him was a delusion, and that I truly didn't know if medication was beneficial or necessary for him.

Joel, though, didn't take my invitation to discuss these topics right away. Instead, he started, hesitatingly and with long periods of silence, to discuss issues with respect to his basic social situation: economy, work, and housing. His parents had given him an ultimatum: either he found some occupation that would take him away from home, at least part of the day, or he found somewhere else to live. In most of our sessions around this time, Joel, in glimpses, expressed how scared he was at the prospect of leaving his parents' home, one way or the other, and he expressed feelings of despair at a sense of living in an utterly meaningless way. He longed to live in a way more like that of other young people, and he started to show an interest in occupational possibilities and spent much time discussing his occupational preferences. To all of this, I responded with ordinary empathic understanding responses. Routinely, though, Joel quickly reverted to a more superficial level of experiencing, or he reverted to silence. Finally, he decided to accept a long-standing invitation to see the hospital's social worker to find out if some of his occupational ideas and wishes could be put into practice. This resulted in his acceptance of a part-time sheltered occupation and he was concomitantly accorded disability benefit.

These arrangements seemed to bring an acceptable daily routine to the way Joel and his parents lived together and to free Joel to discuss other topics. He now started to touch upon his conviction that somebody wanted to kill him and his reasons for this conviction. He wanted to know how I thought about it, which I told him. He didn't delve deeper into his experiences though and if I in any way reached out for them, he withdrew.

Around this time, he asked for twice-weekly sessions, because he felt he needed the support of our conversations to manage his occupation successfully. I was quite surprised at this request, because Joel had continued to seem somewhat fearful and hesitant about our relationship. Only when looking back to the start of our relationship, in the closed ward, could I truly appreciate how much more free and trusting Joel had become. Of course, I accommodated his request.

From this point on, he became a truly voluntary client, albeit still not a very self-expressive one. He talked mostly of things external to himself, in the form of a report on the events of his life since our last meeting, particularly events at work, and being together in silence was still our most frequent way of being together. It was during this phase in the therapy that I first learned about pre-therapy, and applying the contact reflections of pre-therapy helped me greatly in being with him on a more appropriate level of concreteness when I experienced him as being 'out of contact', something that was still predominant at this time. Very gradually, however, his level of experiencing deepened, he became more self-reflective, and I could still more often respond with ordinary empathic understanding responses, i.e. our relationship was developing into an ordinary client-centred therapeutic relationship: I could understand more and more from his inner frame of reference and he seemed more consistently to want me to understand him. This happened concomitantly with his expressing increasingly depressive feelings and ideation. He told me he had always felt that nobody really valued him in anything but a very fleeting and superficial way, and he, too, felt that he was without value, and he doubted his right to exist at all. At times, he expressed wishes about committing suicide and here, too, I stayed with him in the empathic understanding process, although I sometimes did worry very much about the possibility that he would take his own life. At other times, though, he expressed glimmers of hope for himself. He was strengthened in this feeling by some experiences of success at work, and also by realising, with both surprise and relief, that his conviction, that he was the target of a conspiracy to kill him, had started to seem less real to him.

Today he expresses himself with much richer nuances about his experiences in relation to others, not least his parents. He is still hesitant and fearful in his contact with others, but he does find satisfaction in most of the relationships he engages in. His part-time occupation has been exceedingly important in this respect. He continues, though, to be somewhat of a 'loner': he spends much time on his own, but this is now more of a deliberate choice than a necessity. He has also continued to read a lot, he spends much time in sessions telling me what he thinks about some of the stuff he reads, and he uses this as starting points to delve into his own experience.

Reading, and discussing what he reads, has evidently been, and still is, a very important element in his developmental process. Today, though, I don't comment on his reading from my own frame of reference — and he doesn't ask me to, either: I respond to this, as to almost everything else, with empathic understanding responses. The contact reflections of pre-therapy have become much less frequent.

A year ago or so, Joel requested to reduce the frequency of our sessions to once a fortnight and he cancelled one of our appointments because he would rather participate in the summer excursion of his workplace. In sessions, during this year, he has started to weigh the pros and cons with respect to living facilities. He seems to approach a decision to move away from his parents' home, but is unsure whether to move into a flat of his own or accept an offer, from his social worker, to find living facilities which are more sheltered, and where he will live with other young people.

In collaboration with his psychiatrist, with whom he has rare contacts, he has reduced his dose of basic anti-psychotic medication. In addition to this, he administers, on his own, a mild sedative, which he takes on rare occasions when he feels so upset, or overwhelmed by something that has happened, that he can't fall asleep.

He still dreams of, and struggles towards, a 'normal' life for himself, which to him means a life without any contact with anybody connected with psychiatry and without any kind of special protection with respect to economy, occupation, and housing. His current feelings about his progress are ambivalent. He is happy about what has happened, and about the direction of his development, but he is also disappointed about the slowness of the process. By now our relationship has spanned almost six years. In all likelihood, it will endure for several more years to come.

Comments
This example, too, contains many of the characteristics of the process of person-centred interaction and client-centred therapy with psychotic clients as follows.

1. The long-term perspective is typical, with its slow and very gradual development of phases from reluctance (rather extreme in this case) to voluntary. Especially in the start, I often felt like giving up. Looking back at this period today, I regret that I didn't know about pre-therapy at the time: I am sure I'd have felt much more at ease with Joel in a pre-therapeutic relationship and that this would have been more agreeable to him and probably made the first, to me very difficult, phase of reluctance and pre-expressiveness shorter.

On the other hand, the possibility, in the start of our relationship, of my listening, in the presence of Joel, to his favourite music, did lend some sort of 'we feeling' to the relationship, at least for me. Listening to music is a frequent enjoyment of young psychotic people, and it is not an unusual starting point of my relationship with clients like Joel. In Joel's case, I do think it was my silent, non-intruding listening to his music which made it possible for Joel to start to trust me enough to let himself be persuaded by his parents to continue talks with me after his dismissal from hospital. Being together in singing and music seems to be one of the few ordinary ways of being together that do not disappear when people become very psychotic or very senile-demented.

Today, of course, I'm glad I continued the relationship with Joel despite my dismay about it, but, also typically, it is still the case in my relationship with Joel that it is necessary to look back for months, rather than weeks (not to mention single sessions), to realise that progress is taking place. In addition, it is still the case with Joel that his level of expression of his experiencing is generally shallower than that of clients who have started out as ordinary client-centred therapy clients, voluntary and self-expressive. However, my hope and conviction is that Joel's level of expression of his experience will deepen further, in due time, as he slowly actualises his constructive potentials to a still higher degree.

2. The example is also typical in that there will probably be no clear-cut termination of the therapy but rather a continuation on a very elastic schedule and, later, an agreement that Joel can contact me for sessions when he feels like it.

3. Further, the example is typical in that psychotherapy alone won't do it. The superficial improvement of Joel during his stay in hospital had very little, if nothing at all, to do with our relationship. Rather, this improvement was the result of medication and milieu therapy, enabling Joel to control himself better, get a little distance to his delusional experience and learn how to behave to obtain a dismissal from the hospital. It was only much later that Joel started to talk about his delusional experiences in the therapy, and in the beginning, he did this fearful of both re-admittance to hospital and repercussions from his persecutors for disclosing anything about them. After dismissal from hospital, the support and caring of his parents, as well as the help Joel received from the social worker, were important factors in his progress, and so was the good collaboration with respect to medication, which slowly developed between Joel and his psychiatrist. It is my experience, in general, that the psycho-therapeutic process tends to stagnate — or cannot get started — when basic social needs with respect to economy, housing, occupation, and the like are not sufficiently tended to.

4. Another very typical trait is the extremely depressive feelings and attitudes Joel disclosed as his more paranoid experiences diminished. The psychoanalytic writer, Melanie Klein (1952), has described the 'paranoid' and 'depressive' positions, respectively, in the normal development of all infants' object relations. Parents may recognise this or not, but I recognise it very clearly in the therapeutic process with psychotic clients. The expression of depressive experiences normally ushers in a phase of increasing mutuality in the contact with the client, the hesitant start of a more ordinary therapeutic relationship. The Danish psychoanalytic writers, Thorgaard and Rosenbaum (1996), speak of psychoses as the constructive alternative to suicide for very fragile and vulnerable people, and they designate the patient's ability to tolerate depressive experiences without trying to commit suicide, and without an upsurge of paranoid experiencing, as a decisive, progressive turning point in therapy. It is, though, a turning point that is also hard for the therapist to endure, a turning point that puts the therapist's trust in the inherent constructive direction of actualisation to the test. With Joel, as with other clients in this phase, I was very tempted to propose, if not insist on, a re-admittance to hospital as a precautionary measure, because I was very worried that he might try to kill himself. I didn't do it though, and my trust in the core conditions facilitating actualisation of the client's constructive potentials was confirmed: Joel pulled through. In my relationship with Joel, therefore, I acted differently than in my relationship with the psychotically depressed woman I have already written about. There were two main reasons for this.

First, my relationship with Joel was of a very long standing at the time of his depressive period; he had already made progress, so I had reason to believe that our relationship was solid enough to 'hold' him through this extremely painful period. This was different with the psychotically depressed woman, with whom I had just started the therapy, and with whom I found that I had reason to doubt that our relationship had gained significance for her in a way that was strong enough to 'hold' her. (See Winnicot (1987, pp. 43–50 and pp. 240–1) for the concept of the therapeutic relationship as a 'holding' relationship.)

Second, Joel's depressive feelings, attitudes, and experiences were not to nearly the same extent grounded in delusional experiencing: they were not part of an acute psychotic episode. Rather, they had been part of his self-concept for almost all of his life, and there was really no reason to believe that hospitalisation would change that. For Joel, suicidal ideation was, I thought, an element in an existential problem, not a symptom of psychosis.

In addition, and more diffusely, I simply felt convinced that any deviation from non-directively trusting Joel's knowing best what to do about himself and his life would, at that point in time, be tantamount to ruining the therapy process. Had I taken over the process, with proposals for, or insistence on, hospitalisation, I feel convinced that Joel would either have terminated the therapy or allowed himself to 'succumb' to me as an authoritative expert on him, giving up some, at least, of his autonomy. I didn't think that the damage done by Joel's very realistic loss of trust in me, occasioned by my loss of trust in him, would be reparable, as was the case with the psychotically depressed woman.

5. Also rather typical was the process of Joel's parents. When Joel was in the closed ward, they had many talks with Joel's primary nurse and with Joel's psychiatrist, which helped them during the traumatic time when they had their son forcefully committed to the closed ward of a psychiatric hospital. Later, they participated in a supportive and 'psycho-educative' group for relatives of patients suffering from schizophrenia. It was with the support of this group that they finally refused to have Joel staying at home without any activity or occupation outside the home. In the first long time after dismissal from the hospital, they also secured the support of the group with their wish to put quite a pressure on Joel to continue the anti-psychotic medication and to continue seeing me. In short, they became more confident in demanding what they wanted from Joel, in return for allowing him to stay at home with them. I think this process of his parents was beneficial to Joel, even if it was also sometimes a source of frustration for him. After some initial difficulty, his parents also came to accept that I would not share any information about Joel with them.

6. In contrast with what has been described above as rather characteristic of the process with psychotic patients who start out being more or less reluctant in the relationship, the relatively abrupt change to coming somewhat more eagerly to sessions, which Joel demonstrated when he started bringing a bag of books, is not very characteristic. Normally, my impression of how voluntarily clients like Joel attends sessions is much more fluctuating over a rather extended period of time. Characteristic, though, is the fact that I, during this transitional phase between the client's attending reluctantly and the client's attending voluntarily, let myself be directed to my own frame of reference. In Joel's case I did it by commenting on the stuff he had read, as requested, and by answering his questions concerning the diagnosis of schizophrenia. Only later — when the client has become more securely voluntary and self-expressive, when I feel convinced that psychotherapy is what the client wants, and when I experience his inner frame of reference more

continuously — do I endeavour to remain consistently in the empathic understanding response process.

In the preceding two examples, I have predominantly gone into the details of characteristics of the therapeutic process with relatively withdrawn and/or involuntary clients, because they are the ones who are on the fringe of, or outside, the ordinary client population of client-centred therapy. Many psychotic clients, though, are neither reluctant nor involuntary: they start out in therapy as well-motivated as the ordinary client group. With these psychiatric clients, therapy proceeds as with any other clients, with the only difference that they can often be more difficult to understand, and that the use of the contact reflections of pre-therapy is more frequent. I shall therefore not dwell further on the therapeutic work with these clients, but refer the reader to the rich literature on therapy with the more ordinary client population of client-centred therapy.

In addition, I'd like to refer the reader to some of the transcripts of Rogers' therapies with psychotic patients, for example with Jim Brown (Farber et al., 1996, pp. 231–40), and Loretta (ibid. pp. 33–44). These transcripts show how Rogers spontaneously applies — and sometimes does not apply — some of the key principles of work with the psychotic group of patients which have been described in this section. More specifically, they show that the therapist often approaches the patient out of his own desire and interest, and that the therapist often intermingles his tentative, acceptant, empathic understanding responses with contact reflections, when he has no idea what is going on in the client. It therefore seems appropriate that I should conclude this section with an example of how Rogers works with a psychotic patient. This example also gives a vivid sense of how incoherent (to others) and difficult to understand these patients can be. I have made comments between sections of dialogue.

Example: Rogers works with Elaine

The example is an interview Rogers conducted with a teenage girl in a psychiatric hospital. The following two segments of dialogue appear in Brodley and Schneider (2001).

T1a: I've seen you twice now. (C: Uhm hm.) I just thought that I would like to talk with you. I would be interested if you would tell me about yourself and your situation.

Rogers is the one who initiates the contact, and he does this with an offer of interest, not with an offer of help. This is characteristic of the beginning phase of the relationship with many psychotic patients.

The first of many 'sessions' often start in this way.

A short theoretical digression may be appropriate at this point. The therapist offering his interest is, in a very fundamental way, more appropriate for the client-centred therapist than offering his help. Being interested in understanding the client is something the therapist can guarantee the client, whereas he cannot guarantee that he will be of help to the client. He can only hope that this will be the case, and, based on his previous experience and on research, he can find it more or less likely. In a very deep sense, the therapist's conviction of the basic hypothesis of client-centred therapy is put to the test with each new client. A more fitting name for 'client-centred therapy' would therefore, I think, have been 'client-centred understanding', because interest in understanding the client is what fundamentally motivates the client-centred therapist. The therapeutic effect is a welcome by-product of this interest.

C1: Well, my situation is tough.

T1: Your situation is tough. (C: Yeah) Do you want to tell me a little about it?

C2: Well, it's mostly home and with my parents except when other people ... I don't know exactly what happened ...

T2: You're confused why it's so disruptive.

C3: Yes, it is.

T3: But it's hard to tell about.

C4: Yes it is. (T: Uhm hm) I think to drop it is an answer. Just drop it, or something.

T4: That's one possibility is to just drop it. Uhm hm.

C5: Just forget about it.

T5: Ah ... if you could just put it out of mind. (C: Yeah.) Uhm hm. And then sometimes that seems like ...

C6: The only possible thing to do.

T6: The only possible thing to do. You might like to forget it and drop it. But ...

C7: Once you get away with murder, once you get more away with other ...

T7: Is. Uh, that ... and this is your parents you're speaking of? (C: Yes) That when they get away with ...

C8: Or anyone.

T8: Or anyone. (C: Yes) That 'When they get away with murder once, why, boy, then they try it again.'

C9: Yeah. Yeah.

The preceding interaction (from C4 to T8) illustrates, I think, the incoherence that is characteristic of the dialogue with many psychotic patients, and the therapist's continuous 'holding and letting go' of his momentary tentative, empathic understanding of the patient.

T9: Do you feel that's true with your parents?
C10: No, not naturally, 'cause (inaudible) when she got beat up. She's been meddling in other people's affairs.
T10: Uhm hm. And I guess you don't like her when … (C: No, I don't) … she meddles in other people's affairs. That makes you …
C11: Pretty disgusted.
T11: Disgusted. Uhm hm, uhm, hm. (Pause) Could you tell me any more about that?

It seems to me that Rogers at this point (after the pause) may have lost his sense of having an experience of the inner frame of reference of Elaine and that he puts his question to her in an effort to rediscover her inner frame of reference. However, the question is somewhat directive and probing, trying, as it does, to focus Elaine's attention on a particular issue. It might have left her more free to pursue her own process, if Rogers had stayed silent, or if he had made a contact reflection, for example, 'You said you were pretty disgusted' (word-for-word reflection), or 'You've fallen silent' (situational reflection), or both: 'You said you were pretty disgusted and now you've fallen silent'.

C12: Well, it would incriminate me quite a bit.
T12: I see. If you really told, that would … It would kind of incriminate you.
C13: Yes. It would.
T13: Kind of put you in a bad light if you really … (C: Yes it would) told about it.
C14: Except my mother and father.
T14: I see. So you feel you would hardly um, dare tell your side of it because it might incriminate you. You'd rather leave it up to your folks.
C15: Yes (T: Uhm hm, Uhm hm) Does that settle that?

Although Elaine starts to answer Rogers' question, I think she must have felt somewhat pressured by the (very uncharacteristic) directiveness of Rogers' question, since she indirectly signals a wish for the issue to be 'settled'. It can be hard for some near-psychotic and psychotic patients to resist the temptation to say things that they also do not want to say, and sometimes, in the session, they can also feel relief by saying them. At the same time, however, the patient may, for example, carry away feelings of anger or resentment at the therapist for making her tell (see the example of Hannah, p. 135). In addition, the patient may not be able to keep the benevolent picture of the therapist in her mind after the session, but instead becomes more and more convinced that the therapist now values her less for what she has disclosed. Any number of negative reactions to therapist directivity can occur. However, since the patients of psychiatry are generally more difficult to understand than the ordinary client population of client-centred therapy, ideas of deviating from the non-directive attitude tend to cross the mind of the therapist more easily with psychiatric patients, and the temptation to act on these ideas can be harder to resist.

T15: Well, there might be … the thing is that, uh, I guess that settles part of it. But I was thinking that if there was anything that you were willing to tell me that would help me to know you better.

Rogers accepts Elaine's reluctance to continue telling him about this particular issue, and, in a way, starts the interview all over again with a totally open question, which expresses nothing but his interest in getting to know her. This is characteristic of the balancing between the therapist's respect for the patient's wishes, on the one hand, and the therapist's wish to get to know and understand the patient, on the other hand, when the patient is reluctant and it is the therapist who has initiated the contact. Elaine is not a 'client' in the ordinary sense of this word.

C16: Well, my heritage for one thing.
T16: About your heritage.
C17: I feel incriminated myself.
T17: You feel incriminated yourself.
C18: You see (inaudible) my son was in it?
T18: Your son was in it.

As a reaction, I think, to Rogers' previous directive question, and maybe also to his evident wish of continuing the interview, despite her expression of some reluctance, Elaine, in this part of the interview, becomes slightly more withdrawn and difficult to understand. Seemingly having no proper sense of having an experience of Elaine's inner frame of reference, Rogers intuitively and spontaneously empathises with her on the very concrete level of the contact reflections of pre-therapy (the word-for-word reflections in T16,17,18), thereby, in his practice, anticipating Garry Prouty's later development of pre-therapy. These reflections do seem to facilitate Elaine's sense of safety in the relationship from C19 onwards, where she seems to be talking a little more freely about herself and her relationship with her relatives.

C19: Yeah (T: Uhm, hm) My grandmother told me my history and that …
(T: Hmm) She wants me to know her son's history. (Inaudible)
T19: Uhm hm. She brings in her son's history and your parents bring in

your history? Hmm? And that's pretty rough.
C20: Yes it is.
T20: I'm not sure I quite understand that.
C21: Mine isn't any better than his.
T21: Yours isn't any better than his. (C: No) So that in a sense, both histories sort of incriminate each other. (C: Yes) Uhm hm. Hmm. I guess what you're saying is that if the truth came out, or your parents told the whole story it would make it look pretty bad for you. Is that ...?

Rogers again responds to C21 with a word-for-word contact reflection. Then, however, he guesses at Elaine's inner frame of reference in terms of her earlier statements, and in terms of the issue she has expressed reluctance to tell about. It would probably have been preferable for Rogers to just make the contact reflection and follow where she would go from there.

The ensuing segment of dialogue is hard to make sense of because so many statements, particularly Elaine's, are inaudible. I would guess that expressing herself less audibly is Elaine's reaction to Rogers' effort to try to guess at her inner frame of reference. Reluctant patients, like Elaine, may easily experience such an effort as intrusive. It is important to remember that, with psychotic patients, empathic understanding of their inner frame of reference is of relatively less importance than unconditional positive regard as a therapeutic factor, and that with these patients the literal level of the contact reflections of pre-therapy may be a way of expressing unconditional positive regard, which is more safe for the client.

C22: Yes, that would (inaudible).
T22: So you feel that if the (C: History) story came out ...
C23: That would (inaudible).
T23: If the (inaudible).
C24: (Inaudible)
T24: Uhm hm. Uhm hm. But it does seem as though, if the true story came out, you're afraid that, that you'd be put away for life. (C: Uhm hm) Hmm, You must feel that the true story is pretty bad.
C25: The true story is ... (inaudible) and he gets away with everything (inaudible) 'cause I won't have anything to do with it.
T25: I see. So that when he gets out, you're going to have to sort of face up to the truth. (C: inaudible) You won't have anything to do with it.
C26: No. I won't.
T26: So I guess it sounds like you did have something with him in the past. But not in the future you won't.
C27: No, not in the past, present or future, no. (T: Uhm hm.) There's nothing to look forward to.
T27: You really feel there's nothing to look forward to.

....
C42: I do want to stop fighting so my father can (inaudible).
T42: Uhm hm, Uhm hm. That's one of the things you'd like.
C43: Yes I do. And all the way up to my friend's house. (T: Uhm hm)
up to the house and let me clean up. That's what I wanted to do.
T43: The other thing you wanted to do was to clean it up as far as the road.
C44: There will be a highway. (Inaudible) It would be better not to talk
about it. (T: Uhm hm) That's good.
T44: Are there other things you could tell me to help me know you a little
better? 'Cause I don't know anything of your record or ...

I think a response that expressed understanding and acceptance of
Elaine's resistance to talk about this issue (C44) would have been
preferable. Such a response often facilitates the patient's expression
of a wish to discontinue the interview, which the therapist has
initiated. I always immediately accommodate such a request. Often
the first talks last only a few minutes, but it has seemed, to me, to be
important for the patient's feeling of safety in the relationship that I
from the outset signal acceptance of any wishes to discontinue the
interview. I am very aware, with these patients, that I am the one
who initiates the contact, and I do not want the patient to feel that I
impose myself on her. But it surely is one of the really hard balances
to strike right. To the degree that I err, though (which I find it very
easy to do with these often very ambivalent and hard-to-understand
patients), I'd rather err in the direction of the interview being
discontinued too early than too late.

C45: You probably already know.
T45: No. I really don't.
C46: You really don't know me.
T46: No. I really don't know you. Just what you've told me now is what I
know of you.
C47: Mhm. It takes lots of expense and money (inaudible).
T47: It takes lots of expense and money to ...
C48: To carry on such a performance.
T48: Now there I'm not quite sure. You carry on such a performance ...?
C49: Well this is awfully embarrassing. (T: Hmm.) 'Cause my father is
connected to it too. I wouldn't want to say anything to ... (inaudible).
T49: But really, there is something that troubles you and all, but you don't
like to bring it out because it may affect other people and you feel it might
do them ...

In T47 and T48 Rogers again responds with contact reflections and
this seems to facilitate Elaine's contact with herself (in C49), which
enables Rogers (in T49) to make a proper empathic understanding

response (rather than an 'empathic guess'). Elaine, again, seems to respond to this with an increased sense of safety in the relationship, judged by her greater expressiveness in the following, last, segment of the interview.

C50: More harm and no good. More harm as far as my father's mom. (Inaudible) I can't do anything about it. My name and his name (inaudible) (T: Uhm hm) When we went through this as far as the performance, that settled me.
T50: So that you think you've settled.
C51: Yeah. At least I hope it is. 'Cause I know my dad wouldn't make a habit of it.

I think this example with a patient, whose speech seems quite incoherent, and who is very difficult to understand empathically, is a testimony of Rogers' deep, unconditional acceptance of his clients, in this case Elaine. I also find it illuminating that Rogers' sensitivity for, and acceptance of, this psychotic patient seemingly has as a consequence that, apart from a few instances of 'empathic guessing', he often lets go of trying to understand her inner goings on empathically. Instead, he empathises literally, akin to contact reflections, when he seems not to experience her inner frame of reference — several years before Garry Prouty's theoretical development of pre-therapy. Finally, I think, the example illustrates unconditional positive regard as the primary therapeutic agent, and unconditional positive regard being of relatively greater importance as the therapeutic agent with psychotic patients than the ordinary empathic understanding of the client's inner frame of reference.

PATIENTS DIAGNOSED WITH A NEAR-PSYCHOTIC CONDITION

The risk of facilitating actualisation of the client's more destructive potentials

In the psychiatric setting the so-called near-psychotic patients are also variously called 'borderline', 'lower level personality disorder', 'weakly integrated personality disorder', and, within a client-centred framework, Margaret Warner (1991), has written about 'fragile' and 'dissociative' processes in these clients. The term 'near-psychotic' refers to many of these patients' proneness to experiencing psychotic alterations, of relatively short duration, in their perception of reality. Still, the diagnosis, as such, is of no issue to the client-centred therapist.

Much more important is that they are very susceptible to outside influence, and in the extremely protected and more or less paternalistic milieu of a psychiatric hospital, they are prone to react, complementarily, with increasingly immature and dependent behaviours, which can include very impulsive outbursts, self-mutilation and/or short psychotic episodes. Hospital treatment may easily harm them more than help them. It is as if they cannot resist the temptation to turn to ever-greater dependency with all these helpful and caring hospital staff members around. There is a tendency that the more staff members do for the near-psychotic patient, the more they try to be helpful, the more dependent the patient becomes. Great efforts are therefore made to treat them as outpatients, and to keep the duration of unavoidable in-patient treatment as short as possible. When this is not deemed feasible, most often because of self-destructive behaviour, the psychiatric hospital can become an 'insufficient therapeutic context' (Mearns, 1990) for these patients, when they are seen as clients in therapy. This means that the 'pull' of the context towards having the client actualise his less, rather than more, constructive potentials is greater than the reverse 'pull' of client-centred therapy. The risk of this happening is, of course, the greater the more staff members tend to see themselves as experts on these patients.

Near-psychotic patients often pose a true dilemma to the psychiatric system. Society expects psychiatry to protect its patients against physical harm, whether self-inflicted or not. In order to accommodate this expectation, however, by all kinds of protective means, applied with or without force, psychiatry may easily harm patients, particularly near-psychotic patients, psychologically, thereby actually increasing, rather than lessening, the risk of future (self)-destructive behaviour. Psychiatrists are often painfully aware of this dilemma of being damned if they do and damned if they don't, and being the psychiatrist-in-charge for near-psychotic patients can be a very stressful and vulnerable position. In such cases, it becomes very evident that psychiatry, in many ways, reflects the limits of tolerance of a given society, and that the 'critique of psychiatry' is an ethical issue of the whole society, at least as much as it is an issue of the psychiatric system seen in isolation.

The risk of near-psychotic patients actualising their less, rather than more, constructive potentials is considerable, too, when they are treated with methods of psychotherapy that employ directive interventions (psychoanalytic therapy or cognitive-behavioural therapy, for example). These interventions are meant to be helpful, of course, but they may all too easily result in more, rather than less, disturbed behaviour in these clients. In psychotherapy, too, near-psychotic clients seem to adapt complementarily to their therapist behaving as an expert on them, even in minor ways, by surrendering their expertise on themselves and becoming more helpless.

Near-psychotic clients, therefore, more than anybody else, put the competence of the client-centred therapist to the test. They are less resilient to therapist errors and mistakes than is ordinarily the case. For most clients, incomplete or even mistaken attempts at empathic understanding are inconsequential when interspersed unsystematically within a generally empathic context. Such responses can even offer the client a beneficial opportunity to disagree with the therapist. This, however, is not to the same degree true for near-psychotic clients. They are quite sensitive to inaccurate empathic understanding and to rather slight and fleeting instances of therapist expressions of incongruence and conditional regard, and, particularly, they are sensitive to any deviations from the non-directive attitude. Confronted, basically, with any other person's perception of himself as an expert on them, near-psychotic persons tend, to a greater degree than others, to react by engaging in less constructive behaviour and ways of interacting.

In my experience, therefore, the only safe psychotherapy with these clients is *non-directive* client-centred therapy. The theory says that consistently receiving the client with empathic understanding, and thereby expressing one's unconditional positive regard for him, facilitates actualisation of the client's most constructive potentials. With near-psychotic clients, the opposite can easily come true, i.e. if the client is not received in this way, actualisation of the client's more destructive potentials will be facilitated.

In the following section, I'll discuss this in a little more detail.

Near-psychotic clients and unconditional positive regard

In client-centred theory, the therapeutic agent is normally thought to be unconditional positive regard. The 'unconditional' in unconditional positive regard means that *all* client expressions are listened to, understood, and responded to, with equal acceptance. Some expressions or aspects of the client are not valued higher by the therapist than any others. This is of particular importance with the near-psychotic client. These clients tend to express very divergent aspects of themselves at different times and if some aspects are valued higher than others by the therapist, these aspects will typically be those expressed by the client until, sooner or later, their 'opposites' will be expressed in ways that probably are immature, psychotic, and/or dependency-seeking. The 'unconditional' in unconditional positive regard is therefore of major importance with these clients, not only in order to be helpful, as is the case with all clients, but especially in order not to do harm.

The following example is a particularly clear illustration of the way a near-psychotic client reacted with actualisation of her more destructive potentials when confronted with a deviation of mine from the 'unconditional' in unconditional positive regard.

Example: Actualisation of more destructive potentials facilitated by an expression of conditional regard

Lizzie is a near-psychotic client experiencing recurrent, short, psychotic episodes, where she hears voices ordering her to cut her wrists. When this happens, her almost ever-present anxiety amounts to panic, and if she feels alone and unsupported in these situations she will obey the voices and cut her wrists in order to regain some measure of peace. If there is a staff member nearby with whom she can discuss her experiences, she can normally profit from this and calm down without harming herself.

I've had twice weekly sessions with Lizzie for about a month. It is my impression that she is slowly gaining a feeling of safety in our relationship: she is starting to express herself and tell me about her experiences with more nuances, details, and clarity. At about this time the following episode occurs:

The road from the hospital to the nearby village and shopping centre passes through a forest. One day, by accident, I meet Lizzie on the road. She is on her way back to the hospital, and, quite contrary to her habitual rather shabby looks, she now looks gorgeous. She has evidently just left the hairdresser and some fashion shop in the shopping centre. She looks very happy and greets me with a big smile: 'Hi, Lisbeth, what do you think, don't I look nice like this?' And I, quite surprised to see how pretty she can look, respond with: 'Wow, yes, you just look beautiful, what a change!'

We exchange a few more remarks about her 'new looks' and confirm our appointment for the next day before we continue in opposite directions.

At the staff meeting the next morning, I learn that a police search to find Lizzie had been requested a couple of hours after we took leave of each other, because she had not returned to the ward.

She had been found rather quickly, in the forest, not far from the road, with her back leaning against a tree and in a totally apathetic mood. She had cut into both of her wrists with a stone.

In the sessions following this episode, her experiences around it slowly surfaced, facilitated by my consistent staying in the empathic understanding process with her. She told how she had at first felt very pleased with my spontaneous expression of appreciation of the change in her looks. An instant later, though, she had felt overwhelmed by worrying and anxiety-provoking speculations. She felt sure I hadn't really accepted her in our previous sections, because I was disgusted with the way she looked. She also feared that I would now expect her to look her very best in the future, that I'd reproach her for not doing her best if she, again, became more lenient with her looks. Her good spirits had totally disappeared and she started hearing voices ordering her to cut her wrists. In that moment, the distance back to the hospital and safety with a nurse felt too long to her, so she turned into the forest and obeyed orders. In an even slower pace, she expressed her deep disappointment with me. She was used to appreciation and depreciation of her varied behaviours with everybody else, but with me, she had just come to have a little hope that I might accept her no matter what. Then I blew it. She knew she had asked for it by questioning me about my opinion, but still ...

Comments

1. Lizzie was quite right: I blew it. By responding with evident pleasure at her 'new looks' from my own frame of reference, I conveyed conditional regard to her, and, having just started to trust my unwavering acceptance of her, she felt let down by me. I was just like everybody else, wanting her to be a certain way. She was right, too, I did prefer her 'new looks' to her former shabby appearance, but that was totally irrelevant as far as our therapeutic work was concerned. When she, happily, asked 'Don't I look nice?', a much better response from me would have been some empathic understanding response, for example: 'Wow, aren't you just happy to feel so pretty? On top of the world, aren't you?' Alternatively, I might have sung like Maria from 'West Side Story': 'I feel pretty, oh, so pretty ...' I am sure this was the mood of Lizzie in that moment, and she would probably have felt very completely understood by my singing or humming that tune.

2. This example very clearly illustrates the difficulties inherent in accommodating client requests. Lizzie was a self-expressive client who engaged eagerly in the psychotherapy. When she asked me for my opinion, I had the choice between responding with empathic

understanding or, following Lizzie's direction, responding from my own frame of reference. I choose the latter, which, in this instance, was not the better choice.

3. The example also illustrates that one is the client's therapist whether one is inside or outside the consultation room. This was an accidental meeting, and I responded to Lizzie as I'd probably responded to any acquaintance of mine in a similar situation. I was taken somewhat by surprise. I was at that moment fully in my own frame of reference, as I had had no time to adjust my focus to the inner frame of reference of Lizzie in order to receive her fully with acceptant, empathic understanding. I might have made the better choice of response, if Lizzie's question had been her opening comment in a regular session. Therefore, this example also highlights the importance of thinking twice about accommodating requests to be with clients in any other role than the role as a therapist, whether this request is made by the client or by others. The therapist may know that different contexts make different responses likely, but the client may not. It is my experience that it is particularly difficult for near-psychotic and psychotic clients to make this distinction. Whatever the situation, one is their therapist. This is why it is also very important, with these clients, to protect the therapy process by not entering into situations with clients where the therapist's role as therapist cannot be the therapist's highest priority.

4. As a side remark, and more generally, this example also illustrates that praise, which is applied with therapeutic intent in many kinds of helping relationships (and often mistakenly understood as synonymous with the behaviouristic concept of positive reinforcement), can be counter-therapeutic.

Near-psychotic clients and empathic understanding

Unconditional positive regard is communicated as the therapist continuously tries to follow the client in the empathic understanding response process. For this process to be non-directive, the therapist must aim towards *accurate* empathic understanding. This means that the therapist does *not* systematically strive for 'deep' or 'additive' empathy (Mearns and Thorne, 1999, p. 45) or reflections 'at the edge of awareness' (ibid., p. 52). Rainer Sachse (1990, pp. 300–2) has shown that clients typically react with a deepening of their level of experience when the therapist systematically strives for 'deep' reflections and succeeds in this. Such reflections are therefore subtly directive: they do not leave the client to follow his own road, including his own shifts up and down the levels of experiencing. This may not be harmful — and it may even be useful — for the relatively well-integrated client, but it may very well be harmful for the near-psychotic client who is easily overwhelmed and over-stimulated by his inner experiences, and often reacts with increased distortion and denial of experiences in emotionally stressful situations. Aiming towards accurate empathic understanding leaves the client free to deepen or flatten his level of experiencing as he feels like, or is able to do. The near-psychotic client will often flatten his level of experiencing, as a sort of healthy recuperation, before he deepens it again. These clients can therefore talk about the latest fashion in shoes in one moment, only to talk about exceedingly painful experiences the next, and the therapist should follow the client in both directions with equal interest and respect. Alternatively stated, and with expressions borrowed from Godfrey Barrett-Lennard (personal communication, September, 2000), with near-psychotic clients the focus of the therapist will be on 'the thinking' rather than on 'the thinker' more often than is the case with the ordinary client population of client-centred therapy. This is no wonder, when one considers these clients' closeness to a 'psychotic breakdown'. As stated earlier, in psychosis, the experience of oneself as the agent or source of experiences often becomes threatening.

Of course, the therapist's empathic understanding will not always be on the precise level of experiencing of the client. Sometimes it will err in the direction of flattening; sometimes it will err in the direction of deepening. Mostly this is not harmful because it is unsystematic and therefore non-directive; it does not imply that the therapist has a goal for the client, i.e. that the client should deepen his level of experiencing. Raskin (1988, p. 33) differentiates between systematic and unsystematic therapist responses and says that therapists making systematic responses have 'a preconceived notion of how they wish to change the client and work at it in systematic fashion, in contrast to the person-centred therapist who starts out being open and remains open to an emerging process orchestrated by the client'.

There is one definition of empathic understanding which in my opinion better than any other ensures *accurate* (and, by implication, non-directive) empathic understanding, namely the following by Barbara Brodley (2000, p. 4):

> The empathic therapist is not focused on understanding the client's literal words but instead is trying to grasp the meanings that the client seems to intend to be understood by the listener ... The therapist's sole goal in empathic understanding is to acceptantly understand the client in a manner that is likely to result in the client having the experience of being understood.

I have taken this to mean that trying to empathically understand the client is trying to understand what the client wants the therapist to understand. This definition gives the therapist a focus for empathic understanding that is very precise and at the same time very respectful of the level of experiencing of the client. In my opinion, the client-centred therapist should strive for this accurate empathic understanding with all clients in order to remain non-directive and maximally minimise the risk of conveying conditional regard to the client, but as with the 'unconditional' of unconditional positive regard, it is particularly important with near-psychotic clients in order not to do harm.

Example: Following the levels of experiencing of the near-psychotic client

Johnny is 21 years old. He was persuaded by his father to let himself be hospitalised. He was reluctant about the hospitalisation, but, formally, he was a voluntary patient. The occasion for his hospitalisation was a suicide attempt. He had taken an overdose of his father's sleeping pills but his father found him soon enough for his life to be saved. The attempt followed shortly after his first girlfriend, ever, had terminated their relationship of half a year's duration.

Johnny is an only child. He still lives with his father who raised him alone, because his mother died in a car accident a few months after he was born. His father never remarried.

Johnny did reasonably well at school, although he was somewhat of a troublemaker and did not make any close or long-lasting friendships. After school, he started on a couple of educational courses, but he soon dropped out, finding them boring.

He likes to be in the ward, although he does not engage with any interest in the activities of the ward, or in contact with others. He prefers to stay in the lounge, listening to rock music and watching television.

His main complaint is that he does not know what to do: he has no idea what might be interesting and meaningful to him. He feels empty, and he also sometimes feels that both he and the world around him become unreal. Then he can become panicky, he can't tolerate his condition any more, and he feels like doing something desperate, which he often does. For example, he takes a chair and bangs it vehemently into the wall of his room, he bursts out in violently angry verbal attacks on staff members on the slightest provocation, or he goes to the nearby pub and gets himself very drunk. He is convinced that if he could get his girlfriend back everything would be OK. If he cannot, and if treatment does not change things for him, he is convinced that he will try to commit suicide again. As a matter of fact, he is rather convinced that the only thing that will do him any good is getting his girlfriend back; he doesn't really believe he can be helped by any kind of treatment. It is mostly his father who persuades him to accept what he is offered, and, all in all, he seems to be in the hospital mostly because he doesn't know what else to do.

In our talks, he has a 'staccato' rhythm. He engages in dialogue for a while, then he falls silent, and then he takes up the dialogue again, but often on a topic with no seeming relation to the previous one. In the first sessions he talks mostly about his relationship with his girlfriend, about different ways he might try to get her back, about different episodes in the ward and conflicts with some of the nurses, and about not being able to stand his condition any more. In the session from which the following excerpt is taken, he has been considering the possibility of writing a letter to his girlfriend when he stops talking and looks down on the floor, his face turned a little away from me. I have no idea what is going on in him, and I remain silent. Then he looks up and evidently focuses his gaze on some photos on the wallboard in my office.

T: You look at the photos.
J: Yes, is it your dog?
T: Yes.
J: It looks sweet.
T: It is; very sweet.
J: It's a beagle, isn't it? (Seemingly, pleased that he knows.)
T: Yes ... feel pleased to be able to recognise it?
J: Yes ... We used to have a basset; I did a lot of obedience training with him. Have you done that?
T: Oh, yes, if you don't do that with a beagle, it is just all over the place.
J (Laughing): Just like with a basset. (Falling silent again, and looking down on the floor. Then he looks at me.)
J: Do you know what incest is?
T: I know what the word means, but I'm not quite sure if that is what you are asking me?
J: (Quickly looking away from me and down on the floor again): Yes ... No, incest is many things, isn't it?
T: Yes. (I feel I have lost contact with Johnny again.)
(Johnny remains motionless and silent for a while; then he looks out of the window.)
T: You look out of the window.
J: Yes, (looking at me again) aren't you disturbed by all that noise from the birds? (there is a colony of crows in the big trees outside.)
T: No, not really, I'm so used to them, I seldom notice.
J: You know, I ... I don't know ... that question about incest ... I don't know.

*T: There is something about incest bothering you, and maybe it is too hard
to talk about?*
J: Yes. (Falls silent, seemingly thoughtful.)
*J (Very quickly and abruptly, almost spitting it out): It is about my father
and maybe it was incest, I don't know, I don't want to talk about it.*
*T: You just want me to know that you're troubled by something your father
has done that maybe was incest, and you don't want to go into any details
about it?*
*J (With evident relief): Right, maybe later, I just wanted you to know that
this is part of the picture, too.*
*T: It's a relief that I know there are such things bothering you, too, and that
you are not obliged to tell me any details about it?*
J: A huge relief, and maybe we can talk more about it next time?
T: We sure can.

After a short silence, Johnny turned to other subjects. He didn't return
to the issue of incest until three sessions later, when he alluded to
the topic after having told how he had had to give up his plan of
watching television in the lounge, because the only seat left was next
to a male nurse in a small sofa.

Comments
(Since, at this point in our relationship, I felt unsure about how
voluntarily Johnny participated, I'll not refer to him, in the following
comments, as a client but as a patient. Correspondingly, although I
use the term 'therapist', the dialogue exemplifies what I think of as
my person-centred interaction practice rather than my client-centred
therapy practice).

1. The therapist does not in any way try to hold on to, or direct the
patient's attention to, topics which may seem of importance to the
therapist from a theoretical point of view (the question of incest).
Unconditional positive regard is towards the patient's choice of
disclosure as well as to his choice not to disclose.

2. The excerpt exemplifies the therapist's following of the patient up
and down the levels of experiencing: from talk about dogs and birds
to expressions of experiences of here-and-now uncomfortable
feelings concerning ambivalence with respect to disclosure and relief
about having this understood and accepted by the therapist.

3. Again there are a couple of (body) contact reflections, when the
therapist experiences that he has lost contact with the patient. ('You
look at the photos', 'You look out of the window'). As already
mentioned, many near-psychotic patients, particularly the least self-

expressive ones, like Johnny, do experience short psychotic episodes of duration from minutes to a few days. In the interaction, these patients will typically move almost imperceptibly from being 'in contact' to being 'out of contact'. The therapist must be able to follow the patient in these movements by empathising at an appropriate level of abstraction, which sometimes means the very concrete level of the contact reflections of pre-therapy. If the therapist has no experience with pre-therapy, it is difficult not to proceed as if the patient is 'in contact', i.e. as if the therapist experiences the existence of an inner frame of reference of the patient for him to try to understand, which may be mostly his own projection. In doing this, he risks becoming subtly interpretative and directive and therefore potentially harmful. The contact reflections of pre-therapy are very helpful in avoiding this.

4. With this somewhat reluctant patient, the therapist prefers to return to his own frame of reference when requested to do so by the patient (by answering questions about dogs and crows). In doing so, the therapist also respects the patient's external focus. The therapist answers questions and accommodates the patient's more or less outspoken request for talk about the world rather than about his inner experiences. Together with the patient, the therapist focuses on the thinking rather than on the thinker, thereby accepting the level of experiencing of this patient, whose tolerance for experiencing himself as the agent of his own feelings, thoughts, etc. is evidently low. In contrast with the well motivated, more consistently self-expressive client, the therapist's keeping the focus on the patient as the experiencing agent, by staying in the empathic understanding process, also when the patient directs the therapist to the therapist's own frame of reference, might easily over-stimulate, or alienate, the reluctant, near-psychotic patient. This might result in the patient withdrawing further from contact, whether with the world, the therapist, or himself.

5. The excerpt also exemplifies that I have objects in my office which patients may feel safe to inquire about or comment upon if they wish to. They are all objects I feel comfortable to talk with patients about. On the other hand, they are sufficiently neutral, in that they don't spring into people's view and demand their attention the minute they enter my office. Apart from the fact that I like to have these objects in my office, they are meant as potential points of departure for 'small talk', when hesitant and reluctant patients seek a respite from their inner experiences. In addition, they are meant as 'anchors of reality', which is of importance to pre-expressive, psychotic patients. Most of the objects are easily recognisable for

patients as they form part of their own history. A few have an intriguing quality that is easy to express curiosity about. I have no abstract objects of art in my office. Dion Van Werde (1998) has written about the importance of decorating psychiatric wards with objects in which patients can recognise their roots ('anchors of reality') and which offer easy points of departure for sharing experiences. Finally, the way I have decorated my office is meant to strike the best possible balance between the too impersonal and the too personal, between 'I'm an expert authority' and 'I'm a personal friend', between the too cold and the too warm, the too distancing and the too inviting. The person-centred approach is also expressed in the way practitioners decorate rooms and offices where they receive clients and patients.

Near-psychotic clients and congruence

Acceptant empathic understanding demands of the therapist that he is fully present in the moment, i.e. the therapist is congruent. Near-psychotic clients are extremely sensitive to therapist incongruence in one way or another, but most likely, in still more disturbed and disturbing ways, the therapist's limits will be tested when and where he is uncomfortable about them. These clients, more than others, seem to need to feel sure that they cannot become 'too much' for the therapist. It is therefore important that the therapist is aware what is and what is not 'too much' for him, that he accepts and respects his own limits, and that he acts in accordance with his limits when he decides whether he will accommodate a client request or not.

It is hard for me to imagine that therapy with these clients can proceed well if the therapist does not have access to frequent and regular supervision or consultation. Personally, I take part in weekly peer group supervision, and the most time there, by far, is spent helping each other with problems of congruence in relationships with near-psychotic clients. Thus the gain in taking up the challenge of working with near-psychotic clients, to a greater extent than with other clients, is that not only is the client's development facilitated, but so is the therapist's.

The following example illustrates the importance of therapist congruence with near-psychotic clients.

Example: Actualisation of more destructive potentials facilitated by incongruent responses

I have seen Peter in therapy for four years. Sessions have been with various frequencies, from twice a week to once a month, according to Peter's wishes. Peter has a diagnosis of paranoid psychosis, although a long time has passed since his latest psychotic episode. He has been hospitalised many times, always on a fully voluntary basis. When I first knew him, he was rather withdrawn, later he expressed his psychotic experiences more openly, and around the time of the developments described in this example, he is plagued more by suicidal impulses than by psychotic ideation. Looking back, it is evident that he has progressed far in the direction of ' normalcy', which has been his deepest wish all through the years I've known him. Medication has been a necessary evil to him, he has reluctantly accepted disability benefit and he has consistently refused offers of more protected living facilities than his own flat. He has, though, been very motivated to take part in psychotherapy, and, when hospitalised, he has also engaged positively in various kinds of therapeutic and educational activities in the ward. He has artistic talents, and about a year ago he took the very scary step of entering art school. Lately, he has sold a couple of paintings and is now hoping to become more economically independent as an artist. In addition, he is struggling to keep off medication and he feels convinced that his latest hospitalisation, just before he entered art school, is also the last. In sessions, he expresses, variously, his feelings of trust in his ability to lead an independent life, his feelings of loneliness and of being at the periphery of his group of class mates in art school, and his feelings of being a failure as a man because he doesn't know how to relate to women. Such is the context in which he, at the end of a session, asks me if he can phone me between sessions when he becomes scared that he can no longer control his suicidal impulses. Ordinarily, I'd refuse to accommodate such a request, and explain why I don't want to accommodate it (see comment 6, p. 132). Concurrently, I'd respond with empathic understanding of his experience of my refusal to accommodate his wish of his need for protection, and of his wish to avoid hospitalisation or other more evident means of protection (joining a day care centre or frequent visits by a community nurse, for example). In this case, though, without clearly knowing why, and also sensing that I am making the wrong choice, I accommodate his request. During the following days, he does call me, and, among other things, he expresses his gratitude that he can call me like this and his assuredness that these 'phone sessions' will help him get through his current crisis. At the same time, though, the 'phone sessions' become still more frequent, of still longer duration, and Peter seems still more disturbed and suicidal. I, too, feel still more disturbed about the direction our relationship has taken, still more disturbed by a mounting feeling of annoyance at interruptions in my schedule and by a mounting feeling of anxiety that his committing suicide, or not, depends on me.

I realise I need help, and I talk about my problems with Peter in my peer consultation group. The acceptance and understanding I experience in the group helps me clarify that I have identified with Peter's wish to avoid hospitalisation because another hospitalisation would feel like a defeat of my psychotherapeutic abilities. Not long ago, I, and the staff members of the ward where Peter has been hospitalised so many times, shared our pleasure about Peter's progress and the positive effects of psychotherapy since his last hospitalisation, and we prophesised that hospitalisation would probably no longer become necessary. This made it harder for me to accept that still another hospitalisation might be needed. In short, I have identified with one side of Peter's dilemma to the detriment of the other; I have in a sense colluded with him in denial and non-acceptance of his dependency wishes. My empathic understanding of his growing wishes for protection and dependency has been disturbed by my own narcissistic wishes for a therapeutic 'success' and my own wishes to feel helpful, and, as a consequence, I have, quite unrealistically, offered myself as protection.

The next time Peter calls, I am able to discuss these issues with him with acceptance of us both and with concurrent empathic understanding of his own feelings of being a failure because he once again wishes protection. He also discloses that he actually did have a sense that I did not feel wholly comfortable about our agreement that he could phone me when he felt he wanted to do so, and this has made him feel quite unsafe in our relationship. Therefore, when I make it clear to him that I will terminate our 'phone sessions' routine, he reacts with mixed feelings of disappointment, relief, and anxiety about what to do now, when he feels hopeless and suicidal. He resolves to make an appointment with his psychiatrist with whom he discusses medication and hospitalisation. The result is that he becomes a day-patient in his 'old' ward twice a week on the days he is not in art school, and I resume ordinary sessions with him once a week. In these, he speaks mostly of his experiences in art school, and after a couple of months he feels better accepted in his class, with a sense of belonging that he enjoys very much. He then stops his day-patient routine without any serious upsurge of suicidal impulses.

Comments

1. Psychiatric clients and, in my experience, especially near-psychotic clients, make all sorts of requests of their therapists. Time and again, I have had the experience that therapy in effect comes to a halt, and clients get worse, if the therapist makes decisions with respect to these requests that he does not feel wholly comfortable with. Near-psychotic clients are very sensitive to therapist incongruence and the therapist not being fully present with them. They seem to become

more helpless under the burden of feelings of anxiety about being rejected by the therapist and about being 'too much' for the therapist, and they'll typically continue becoming still more helpless until the therapist regains his balance and realises that the client has, actually, become 'too much'. In this respect, the above example is very typical.

2. The example is also typical in the sense that it is the narcissistic wishes of the therapist, and his wishes to feel helpful, that contaminate the therapy process. Working with these clients is mostly a very long-term and inconspicuous affair, for long stretches of time nothing seems to happen, sometimes the client's condition deteriorates, and, as a whole, progress is slow and insidious, often in the form of 1 step forward and 0.9 steps backwards. Looking back over a sufficiently long time period, the therapist can notice progress in details in the quality of contact with the client and in the level of the client's experience process in sessions, but others, maybe even including the client, often ignore this kind of progress. With psychiatric clients, there are not many conspicuous changes as a result of psychotherapy, nothing like, for example, the sometimes-overnight disappearance of psychotic symptoms as a result of medication. On the contrary, an intensification of psychotic symptoms can sometimes accompany productive psychotherapeutic work. The work of the psychotherapist mostly goes unnoticed, and it is therefore important that the therapist is not burdened by pressing narcissistic wishes or wishes to feel immediately helpful. These wishes of the therapist must be satisfied in other areas of work. As stated earlier, working exclusively with long-term therapy with psychiatric clients is therefore not a good idea.

3. Further, this example illustrates a typical core conflict of many psychiatric clients: the dependence/independence conflict. Many psychiatric clients have never experienced being safe in a dependency relationship with significant others. For a myriad of reasons, they have developed a 'counter-dependent' self-concept, giving up, and denying or distorting, wishes for dependency too early or too abruptly. They typically feel the stigmatisation as a psychiatric patient very clearly and very painfully, and they'll sometimes undertake very unrealistic actions in their struggle to become independent of the psychiatric system, and the sooner the better. Some of these clients have a very hard process to go through, in coming to accept their wishes for dependence fully (as in, for example, taking up sheltered living facilities) before they can slowly develop in the direction of true independence. With the stress put on promoting independence and autonomy in the general theory of client-centred therapy, this process can be hard on the therapist, too. The therapist can easily come to feel

a failure, as a client-centred therapist, when the client's process is in the direction of more protected ways of living rather than in the direction of more independent ways of living. (See also the therapy excerpt with Lillian, p. 75).

4. In addition, the example illustrates the importance of distinguishing clearly between understanding and accepting wishes for dependency, on the one hand, and accommodating or satisfying them, on the other hand. Most psychiatric clients typically receive several of the services psychiatry has to offer, not just psychotherapy. Many psychiatric services are geared to accommodate, or satisfy, client wishes for dependency, but if psychotherapy becomes one of these, it loses its raison d'être. Furthermore, it is totally unrealistic that the therapist should be able to offer the protection of, say, hospitalisation, sheltered living facilities or sheltered educational facilities, visits by community psychiatric nurses, etc. In the example, the risk of the client committing suicide increased the longer the therapist colluded with the counter-dependent self-concept of the client, because the client did not, in reality, have his wish for protection and care relevantly accommodated and satisfied. This first happened when he was admitted as a day patient.

5. The example also illustrates the importance of good consultation or supervision. Time and again, the therapist will want a place of his own where he feels safe to explore, for example, troubling, albeit unclear, feelings of not being fully congruent in his relationship with a client. No therapist, however competent or experienced, can avoid getting into situations where he feels uncomfortable with his client, and with the 'difficult' clients of psychiatry, the relevance of consultation or supervision is even more obvious. Consultation or supervision is an important forum for the therapist's own development, both professionally and personally. In the United Kingdom, for example, life-long supervision is obligatory. Such is not the case in my country, Denmark, although, fortunately, it is becoming the rule rather than the exception, on a voluntary basis.

6. When clients make requests of me, like Peter's, I ordinarily tell them that I'd feel uncomfortable accommodating it, because, whether realistic or not, I'd feel overburdened and anxious at a sense of being responsible for their protection, and, further, that I'd not feel comfortable about the possibility of having other appointments disturbed. I'd take care to take the full responsibility for my refusal, by stating it clearly in personal terms, from my own frame of reference. Most importantly, I'd not question the wisdom of the client's request by refusing to accommodate it with reference to what

might, or might not, be helpful to the client. I'm not an expert on the client, but I'm an expert on myself. This, and responding empathically to the client's experiences concerning these issues, leads, of course, to the client finding other ways to resolve his dilemma. Sometimes he finds that his need for protection has disappeared or diminished by discussing it. Sometimes I accommodate a request to prolong a session to give the client and myself sufficient time for such a discussion, or I find the first time possible for an extra session. Sometimes we agree on a few, frequent, telephone contacts at specified times that suits my schedule, or we agree on sessions with intervals that are more frequent. Sometimes the client finds that he needs more help and protection than I can satisfy, or of another kind than I can satisfy. If I have been sufficiently comfortable with my own limits, and, at the same time, sufficiently acceptant and empathic towards his wishes for protection, he will then, ordinarily, change his request of me to a fruitful consideration of other means of protection, ranging from hospitalisation to, for example, a weekend at his grandparents', or a consultation with a psychiatrist to discuss medication.

Since the above example has dealt with the importance of the therapist feeling confident and comfortable with his own limits, this might be an appropriate occasion for a short digression into the issue of violence and limits. Patients in psychiatric hospitals, and, particularly, in the closed wards of psychiatric hospitals, display relatively more violent behaviour than the population at large. It is, though, extremely rare for psychotherapists, working in psychiatric hospitals to be exposed to violence from their clients, probably because psychotherapists, of any school, are rarely involved in the managerial and administrative aspects of the patients' treatment. In my career of almost 30 years I've only twice been exposed to violence from clients. Still, the issue is sometimes discussed among psychotherapists, because, now and again, they have the experience that their client can hardly contain his aggressiveness. In addition, for the client-centred therapist, the questions of unconditional positive regard and non-directivity are at stake.

In my experience, the only option for the client-centred therapist is to get up and leave at the first display of violent behaviour. The client may, of course, express himself as aggressively as he wishes, in words, towards the therapist, but the therapist must protect himself against becoming a victim to actions of violence from clients, as from anybody else. The client-centred therapist will not interfere with the client, will not try to make him behave differently, but will instead leave, with the intention of finding someone with the necessary resources to deal competently with the client without anyone being harmed. The therapist does this to protect himself, and, by avoiding a confrontation, he also safeguards his capacity to accept the client by taking care that nobody, including himself, is victimised by this outburst of client violence. Having limits for what one will tolerate from another person is not the same as not accepting that person as he is. One accepts the winter rain, so one can feel comfortable with it, by using an umbrella to avoid getting freezing wet. The first time I was exposed to violence from a client, many years ago, I was paralysed and did not behave very rationally. The second time, years later, when I had clarified the above 'emergency rule' to myself, I was much more satisfied with my behaviour in the situation: the client, in mounting anger, took some papers from my table, crushed them hard, and threw them across the room. I rose immediately to leave, but before I reached the door, the client asked me to, please, come back — he regretted his behaviour, and it would not happen again. I returned, it didn't happen again, and in the ensuing dialogue, the client used the incident as a point of departure for calm self-exploration, and my acceptance of him had suffered no harm.

Near-psychotic clients and non-directivity

As already mentioned, I regard the therapist being securely contained by the non-directive attitude as a 'sine qua non' of client-centred therapy. This aspect of client-centred therapy becomes particularly important with near-psychotic clients, because the risk of directive interventions having negative consequences seems greater with these clients than with others.

The question whether the non-directive attitude is essential for therapy to be called client-centred is a hotly debated question by therapists identifying themselves as client-centred or person-centred. Personally, the non-directive attitude is absolutely essential to me, because I think it follows logically from the hypothesis of the existence of the actualising tendency and the hypothesis of the core conditions being not only necessary, but also sufficient, for client growth (Sommerbeck, 2002a). Others, however, who identify themselves as person-centred therapists, do not agree with this (see for example Edwin Kahn, 1999). Be that as it may, a psychotherapist who is not motivated and contained by the non-directive attitude should, according to my experience, very carefully diagnose and evaluate clients in order not to risk exposing near-psychotic clients to potentially harmful (albeit meant to be helpful) directive interventions. Diagnosing is certainly not in the tradition of client-centred therapy, but it is necessary if the non-directive attitude is not adhered to. Near-psychotic clients are very hard to identify. Although they are frequent clients of the psychiatric system, they can show up anywhere: in private practices, different kinds of mental health agencies, university clinics, etc., presenting themselves as regular crisis clients, as clients with existential problems, or as clients with a symptomatology that is indistinguishable at first from that of the better integrated client. The fragility of the client is often first realised when the client engages in still more (self)-destructive behaviours, and the harm has already been done. Non-directivity is, therefore, necessary to avoid diagnosing and to avoid doing harm.

Dave Mearns (1994, pp. 80–3) writes that a characteristic feature of these clients is their externalised locus of evaluation, and I quite agree with that. As a matter of fact, they seem, in order to have dependency wishes satisfied, to be masters at sniffing out the conditional regard, which they also oppose in order to have independency wishes satisfied. The consistent, non-directive, empathic following, which maximally minimises the risk of conveying conditional regard, is, therefore, necessary for them to struggle constructively with their conflict as an internal conflict. Deviations from this non-directive practice are experienced as conditional regard of one or the other side of the conflict, or as conditional regard of the struggle itself. This will, typically, result in an externalisation of the conflict, which they will then experience (and not without reason) as taking place between themselves and the therapist.

The last example of therapy with near-psychotic clients will therefore be an illustration of the negative consequences of a — meant to be helpful — directive intervention.

Example: Actualisation of more destructive potentials facilitated by a directive intervention

Hannah is 33 years old. She has a long history of impulsive, self-destructive behaviour in stressful situations. She cuts her wrists, swallows sharp objects, overdoses on tranquillisers, etc. She is hospitalised as a consequence of one of these self-destructive episodes and seems to profit from the various activities she is engaged in, including psychotherapy. The following excerpt is from the sixth session with Hannah.

Hannah has spent most of this session talking about the events of the week, listing them without much reference to her thoughts and feelings about them. Towards the end of the session, after a rather long pause, she starts talking about the death of her mother when she, Hannah, was in her teens.

H: It was awful. I've tried to forget about it, but I can't. It feels so bad, I don't know what to do about it, somehow it's always with me, but I've never really talked about it before.
T: Maybe you'd like to try to talk a little about it now? To say a little more about that bad feeling?

(Although very tentatively formulated, this is a directive, probing question. The therapist thinks that it may do the client some good to focus on her current feelings and sensations with respect to her mother's death many years ago. The tone of voice of the therapist, and the way he formulates his question, does express understanding and acceptance of the client's painful feelings, and also that this may be hard to talk about, but the wish to forget about it is ignored.)

H: She died of cancer. It took a very long time. Towards the end her face was ... not right ... it ... it ... (obviously uncomfortable and distressed, fighting with tears) ... it just looked awful, I couldn't bear to look at her.
T: You wanted so much to be close to her, look at her, but it was horrible to do so.
H (between sobs of crying): Yes, I've felt so guilty about it, I just turned away, didn't look at her, she looked too hideous, her eyes were all swollen ... I never kissed her goodbye ... she smelled ...
T: She was just too abhorrent to be close to, to touch and kiss and you've blamed yourself for feeling like that ... and, telling about it, it hurts so awfully much.
H: Yes ... (crying desolately for a while, then rather abruptly, and surprisingly to the therapist, she takes a grip on herself) ... It's too silly to cry about now, it's such a long time ago, and it can't be changed.
T: Annoyed with yourself that you cannot just let bygones be bygones.
H: Yes, that's right, there's no point in dwelling on the past − I do feel a little relieved though.
T: Relieved and annoyed − well, I think time is about up for today.
(After a few small-talk remarks, Hannah leaves.)

The next day the therapist is informed that shortly after the end of the session, Hannah swallowed three sewing needles and was brought to the intensive care unit of the nearest general hospital.

Comment
The emotions stimulated by the successful attempt of the therapist to have the client explore her feelings concerning the death of her mother were evidently more than the client could tolerate. In a later session it became clear that anger at the therapist for having 'forced' her to talk about her mother's death had been the most troubling feeling.

An inaccurate, or rather, incomplete tentative empathic understanding response, which only demonstrated the therapist's understanding of the client's pain, and not of the client's wish to forget about the pain, might easily have been followed by the same sequence of events as the directive, probing question. This is because such an incomplete response would probably be an expression of the therapist's bias that 'deeper is better', i.e. it would be an expression of conditional regard.

Doing no harm

As can be concluded from the above, the sum total of my experience with near-psychotic clients is that the 'first amendment', that of doing no harm, comes to the foreground with these clients in a more radical way than with other clients. To the extent that the therapist succeeds in 'doing no harm', he will probably be helpful. It is of interest, I think, that even within psychoanalytic circles, voices are heard advocating a non-directive approach to therapy with near-psychotic clients. Dawson and MacMillan (1993, p. 57) propose what they call a 'no-therapy therapy' with the intention of 'doing no harm'. By this, they mean a non-directive and technique-free approach, somewhat along the lines of client-centred therapy, although they seem ignorant of the existence of client-centred therapy, at least they do not refer to Rogers, or to any other client-centred authors. In addition, as the name 'no-therapy therapy' implies, their approach is without any understanding of the deeper implications of the theory of client-centred therapy. They seem to regard a 'no-technique therapy' as a 'no-therapy'. Still, 'doing no harm' is, in my experience, the relevant heading for the conditions these clients need in order to develop constructively rather than destructively, progressively rather than regressively. These conditions are best ensured by non-directive client-centred therapy, i.e. by the fully present therapist receiving his client with unconditional positive regard in the empathic understanding response process.

PART FOUR
CULTURAL DIFFERENCES, THE
CRITIQUE OF PSYCHIATRY, AND
ANOTHER PERSPECTIVE

This book has been written from the vantage point of a small (70 beds), Danish, public, psychiatric hospital, and the community psychiatric service associated with it. Like psychiatry all over the western and westernised world, the thinking of staff members is dominated by the philosophy of the medical model. However, there is also quite a high degree of interest in, openness to and respect for, other approaches and ways of thinking, when compared with many other Danish psychiatric hospitals. The drawback of this book, therefore, may be that it does not fully take into account the difficulties client-centred therapists experience with psychiatry in other parts of the world. Furthermore, it may not fully acknowledge that in some places it may be impossible for client-centred therapists to practise in psychiatric contexts, because the philosophy of the medical model is the only philosophy tolerated.

I'd like to illustrate the vast differences in psychiatry, even within the western world, with a couple of striking research results:

1. The Norwegian psychiatrist, Einar Kringlen (1990), is the author of a textbook of psychiatry which is one of the most widely read at the medical faculties of Scandinavian universities. In this book (p. 596), he concludes his survey of major epidemiological research studies about the correlation between social status and psychiatric disorders as follows:

> It is evident that the correlation between social status and mental diseases is greatest in countries with large class differences and social insecurity. It is of interest, therefore, that while population surveys from USA and Canada show a clear correlation between social status and mental disease, with increasing frequency on lower social levels, such a correlation is not found in a population survey from the Scandinavian countries. This could indicate that the welfare model of these countries has a protective effect. (my translation)

This result, I think, casts a very illuminating light on the way differences between even rather closely related countries, and particularly differences in the social and health security/solidarity policies of these countries, influence the psychiatric 'look' of a country.

2. In their paper about the 'Soteria Berne' project, Ciompi et al. (1992)

document that it is possible to help schizophrenic patients without, or with very restricted use of, anti-psychotic medicine, the so-called neuroleptics. In this connection, the doses of neuroleptics used in the Soteria Berne project were compared with the doses normally used in European countries and America, respectively. Ciompi et al. write (p.148) that the Soteria Berne project used one third of the normal European doses, and about one fifth to one tenth of the normal American doses.

My guess is that this, partly at least, reflects the greater influence, as compared with Europe, of the pharmaceutical industry on the health system in America and thereby the greater trust of the majority of Americans in the fact that the 'free market' also applies to the pharmaceutical industry.

From discussions with colleagues from many parts of the world, I have become aware of other cultural differences in the practices of psychiatry, which can make a difference with respect to the possibilities for client-centred therapists to practise within the context of psychiatry. Tendencies towards 'managed care' and 'manualised therapy' , which are antithetical to the philosophy of client-centred therapy, seem much more widespread and dominant in the UK and North America than they do in continental European countries. In addition, to the degree these tendencies exist in a country like Denmark, for example, they do so in a more modified and less extreme form, which does leave room for other approaches.

Another difference is the traditional role of clinical psychology in a country's psychiatric system. Many, maybe even most, psychotherapists working in psychiatric contexts in Western countries are clinical psychologists. However, in Great Britain, for example, clinical psychologists have traditionally come from the behavioural school of psychology, and in the context of psychiatry they have, furthermore, often been more engaged with psychometric studies and testing than with psychotherapy. In the Scandinavian countries, for example, the opposite is the case, i.e. the major part of the work of a clinical psychologist in the psychiatric systems of these countries is traditionally taken up by psychotherapy. This means that although the predominant psychotherapeutic influences in these countries are psychoanalytic and cognitive-behavioural, the clinical psychologist does not have to forge a role for himself as a psychotherapist before he can start forging a role for himself as a client-centred therapist.

The aspect of psychiatry, which I, personally, find most troubling, is the right and obligation of psychiatry to intervene forcefully in certain legally specified circumstances. I think all western and westernised countries have legislation for the use of force in psychiatry, i.e. legislation about circumstances when people can be, and are, compulsorily admitted to, and detained in, a closed psychiatric ward, and compulsorily treated.

This legislation, together with other kinds of legislation, mark the limits of tolerance of the country in question; limits which should, of course, consistently be an issue of open, democratic, political discussion and debate. This, however, does not seem to be the case with legislation about the use of force in psychiatry to quite the same extent as it is the case with other kinds of legislation. The reason for this, as I see it, is the surrendering of power to psychiatry by the given country's insistence that this legislation is for the benefit of the person who is submitted to this use of force. Alternatively stated, the reason is the given country's authoritarian attitude to the expertise of the medical model, and the given country's collective denial that its limits of tolerance are narrower than publicly admitted. People sentenced to prison are not told that this sentence is issued for their own sake. People sentenced to psychiatry are told exactly that, and in my experience with most of the clients I have known, who have had such a sentence, this is by far the most humiliating and traumatising aspect of receiving such a sentence. Treating others with force, against their own will, is one thing, but telling them, at the same time, that it is for their own sake, is, in my opinion, both dishonest and hypocritical, and for the persons submitted to such treatment, it amounts to being confronted with a true 'double bind'.

The list of cultural differences in, and other aspects of, the practice of psychiatry, which can make it more or less difficult to practise as a client-centred therapist in this context, could, of course, be further extended. However, the intention with this section is neither a cross-cultural, comparative, study of psychiatry and its use of the psychotherapeutic treatment modality, nor a general critique of psychiatry. The intention is to illustrate, and acknowledge, by a few examples, why the practice of client-centred psychotherapy will prove much more difficult in some psychiatric contexts than in others. In some such contexts, it may even prove impossible.

One factor, though, which militates against the approach of client-centred therapy becoming more widespread in psychiatry does not come from psychiatry but from the community of client-centred therapists itself. It is the traditional anti-psychiatric stance of many practitioners dedicated to the person-centred approach, a perspective on psychiatry originating with writers like Cooper (1967) and Szasz (1961, 1987). Pete Sanders and Keith Tudor (2001) are contemporary authors who represent this tradition of the person-centred approach beautifully.

When one looks upon psychiatry from the outside, I am, to a very large extent, in agreement with the general person-centred critique of psychiatry, although I do think I discern a tendency, in this critique, to see psychiatry as an 'enemy' or 'an ogre', which I find counterproductive with respect to any intention to humanise the psychiatric system. Anyway, whether this impression of mine corresponds to reality or not, I do find it very important to distinguish between psychiatry as it looks from without, and psychiatry as it looks from within. The outside perspective is necessarily a generalisation, an abstract critique of a 'system' and 'its' practices, but the inside perspective is populated with individual psychiatrists, psychiatric nurses, social workers, etc., who are truly doing the best they know how to be of help to the patients, just as I am. It is, in my opinion, inappropriate, out of line with the philosophy of the person-centred approach, and harmful for the relationship — and it may in the end be harmful for patients — to meet these individuals with a judgemental critique of their individual practices. In addition, if the client-centred therapist, from a position of 'knowing the right way', criticises the practices of individual psychiatrists, nurses, etc., towards one of his own clients, he puts himself in the position of an expert on his client, and thereby he risks jeopardising the therapy process with this client.

This does not mean that a client-centred therapist, who works in a psychiatric context, cannot voice his critique of the practices of the psychiatric system. This can be done in all kinds of meetings, conferences, and so on, where these practices are discussed theoretically and in general. It is in my opinion unwise, though, to voice this critique, or use it as a dominant guideline, in discussions concerning the concrete decisions and practices of individual staff members with respect to individual patients. In such discussions, the philosophy of the person-centred approach should be the main guideline (see p. 9ff). If the client-centred therapist meets individual employees in the psychiatric system as 'ogres', he will, naturally, be expelled. If he meets them as persons, he will be welcomed.

Although I acknowledge the difficulties inherent in working as a client-centred therapist within psychiatry, and although I agree with much of the critique of psychiatry, I am also worried that the predominant anti-psychiatric stance among client-centred therapists can deter client-centred therapists of the future from seeking work in psychiatric contexts. They might feel that seeking such work would mean 'crossing over to the enemy', be an act of unfaithfulness to their dedication to the person-centred approach, and an act of betrayal of the approach. They might feel that they would have to compromise their basic philosophy of life and ways of thinking about therapy and human nature, if they sought employment within psychiatry.

One of my intentions, with writing this book, has been to show that this need not be so. I hope I have succeeded in demonstrating that the anti-psychiatric stance need not be the only perspective of client-centred therapists with respect to psychiatry. I hope I have clarified that there can also, alongside a more or less critical, outside, perspective, exist an inside perspective which can, in the spirit of the person-centred approach, facilitate actualisation of the more constructive potentials of all the inhabitants of the psychiatric landscape, be they patients, staff members, or the therapist himself.

REFERENCES

Bozarth, J. (1990): The essence of client-centered therapy. In G. Lietaer, J. Rombauts, and R. Van Balen (eds): *Client-Centered and Experiential Psychotherapy in the Nineties*. Leuven: Leuven University Press.

Bozarth, J. (1998): *Person-Centred Therapy: A Revolutionary Paradigm*. Ross-on-Wye, UK: PCCS Books.

Brodley, B. (1996): Empathic understanding and feelings in client-centred therapy. *The Person-Centred Journal, 3* (1).

Brodley, B. (1998): Criteria for making empathic responses in client-centred therapy. *The Person-Centred Journal, 5* (1).

Brodley, B. (1999): Reasons for responses expressing the therapist's frame of reference in client-centred therapy. *The Person-Centred Journal, 6* (1).

Brodley, B. (2000): Empathic understanding: observations of a client-centred practice. Paper presented at the International Conference for Client-Centred and Experiential Psychotherapy, Chicago.

Brodley, B. T. and Schneider, C. (2001): Unconditional positive regard in the verbal behaviour of client-centred therapy. In P. Wilkens and J. Bozarth (eds.): *Unconditional Positive Regard: Rogers' Therapeutic Conditions: Evolution, Theory and Practice*, pp.155–72. Ross-on-Wye, UK: PCCS Books.

Cain, D. (1989): The paradox of nondirectiveness in the person-centred approach. *Person-Centred Review, 4* (2), 123–131.

Ciompi, L., Dauwalder, H., Maier, C., Aebi, E., Trütsch, K., Kupper, Z. and Rutishauser, C. (1992): The pilot project 'Soteria Berne'. Clinical experiences and results. *British Journal of Psychiatry, 161* (suppl. 18), 145–53.

Cooper, D. (1967): *Psychiatry and Anti-Psychiatry*. London: Tavistock.

Dawson, D. and MacMillan, H. (1993): *Relationship Management of the Borderline Patient: From Understanding to Treatment*. New York: Bruner/Mazel.

Deleu, C. and Van Werde, D. (1998): The relevance of a phenomenological attitude when working with psychotic people. In B. Thorne and E. Lambers (eds): *Person-Centred Therapy: A European Perspective*, (pp. 206–215). London: Sage.

Dilthey, W. (1894): Ideen über eine beschreibende und zergliedernde Psychologie. In: *Gesammelte Schriften V*, p. 143 ff. Stuttgart, B. G. Teubner, 1957.

Farber, B. A., Brink, D. C. and Raskin, P. M. (eds.) (1996): *The Psychotherapy of Carl Rogers: Cases and Commentary*. London: Guilford Press.

Kahn, E. (1999): A critique of nondirectivity in the person-centered approach. *Journal of Humanistic Psychology, 39* (4).

Kershaw, I. (2000): *Hitler*. London: Penguin.

Kirschenbaum, H. and Henderson, V. (1989): *Carl Rogers: Dialogues*. Boston: Houghton.

Klein, M. (1952): Some theoretical conclusions regarding the emotional life of the infant. In M. Klein (1988): *Envy and Gratitude* (pp. 61–93). London: Virago.

Kringlen, E. (1990): *Psykiatri*. Oslo: Universitetsforlaget (University publishing company).

Lambers, E. (1994): The person-centred perspective on pychopathology. In D. Mearns (1994): *Developing Person-Centred Counselling* (pp. 105–20). London: Sage.

Lindley, D. (1996): *Where Does the Weirdness Go?* New York: Basic Books.

Mahler, M. S., Pine, F., and Bergman, A. (1975): *The Psychological Birth of the Human Infant.* New York: Basic Books.

Mearns, D. (1990): The counsellor's experience of success. In D. Mearns and W. Dryden (eds.): *Experiences of Counselling in Action* (pp. 97–112). London: Sage.

Mearns, D. (1994): *Developing Person-Centred Counselling.* London: Sage.

Mearns, D. and Thorne, B. (1999): *Person-Centred Counselling in Action.* London: Sage.

Morato, H. (1991): Pré-contato com a Pré-terapia do Dr. Garry Prouty. *Boletim Paulista da Abordagem Centrada na Pessoa,* (12), 3–4.

Patterson, C. H. (1995): A universal system of psychotherapy. *The Person-Centered Journal,* 2 (1), 54–62.

Patterson, F. G. P. and Cohn, R. H. (1990): Language acquisition by a lowland gorilla: Koko's first ten years of vocabulary development. *Word, 41* (2), 97–143.

Polkinghorne, J. C. (1984): *The Quantum World.* London: Penguin.

Pörtner, M. (2000): *Trust and Understanding: The Person-Centred Approach to Everyday Care for People with Special Needs.* Ross-on-Wye, UK: PCCS Books.

Prouty, G. (1994): *Theoretical Evolutions in Person-Centered/Experiential Therapy: Applications to Schizophrenic and Retarded Psychoses.* Westport: Praeger.

Prouty, G. (2002): Humanistic psychotherapy for people with schizophrenia. In D. Cain and J. Seeman, J. (eds.): *Humanistic Psychotherapies: Handbook of Research and Practice.* Washington, DC: American Psychological Association, 579–601.

Prouty, G. and Cronwall, M. (1990): Psychotherapeutic approaches in the treatment of depression in mentally retarded adults. In A. Dosen and F. Menolascino, (eds.): *Depression in Mentally Retarded Children and Adults.* Leiden, the Netherlands: Logon Publications, pp. 281–93.

Raskin, N. (1988): What do we mean by person-centred therapy? Paper presented at the meeting of the Second Association for the Development of the Person-Centred Approach, New York.

Rogers, C. (1951): *Client-Centered Therapy.* Boston: Houghton Mifflin.

Rogers, C. (1957): The necessary and sufficient conditions of therapeutic personality change. *Journal of Consulting Psychology, 21* (2).

Rogers, C. (1959): A theory of therapy, personality, and interpersonal relationships as developed in the client-centered framework. In E. Koch (ed): *Psychology: A Study of a Science,* Vol. 3. New York: McGraw-Hill.

Rogers, C. (1961): *On Becoming a Person.* London: Constable.

Rogers, C. (1975): Empathic: An unappreciated way of being. *The Counselling Psychologist, 5* (2).

Rogers, C. (1986): Reflections of feelings. *Person-Centred Review, 1* (4).

Rogers, C., Gendlin, E., Kiesler, D. and Truax, C. (1967): *The Therapeutic Relationship With Schizophrenics.* Wisconsin: University of Wisconsin Press.

Sachse, R. (1990): Concrete interventions are crucial: The influence of the therapist's processing proposals on the client's intrapersonal exploration in client-centred therapy. In G. Lietaer, J. Rombauts, and R. Van Balen (eds): *Client-Centered and Experiential Psychotherapy in the Nineties* (pp. 295–308). Leuven: Leuven University Press.

Sanders, P. and Tudor, K. (2001): This is therapy: A person-centred critique of the contemporary psychiatric system. In C. Newnes, G. Holmes and C. Dunn, (2001): *This is Madness Too: Critical Perspectives on Mental Health Services,* Chapter 14. Ross-on-Wye, UK: PCCS Books.

Shlien, J. M. (1961): A client-centered approach to schizophrenia: First approximation. In A. Burton (ed.): *Psychotherapy of the Psychoses* (pp. 285–317). New York: Basic Books.

Sommerbeck, L. (2002a): Person-centered or eclectic: A response to Kahn. *Journal of Humanistic Psychology, 42* (2), 84–7.

Sommerbeck, Lisbeth (2002b): The Wisconsin Watershed — Or the Universality of CCT. *The Person-Centered Journal*. Volume 9, Number 2, pp. 140-157.

Sommerbeck, Lisbeth (2003): A Case for Non-Directivity. Paper presented at the PCE conference in Egmond an Zee, Holland.

Stern, D. N. (1985): *The Interpersonal World of the Infant*. New York: Basic Books.

Szasz, T. (1961): *The Myth of Mental Illness*. New York: Harper.

Szasz, T. (1987): *Insanity: The Idea and its Consequences*. New York: Wiley.

Teusch, L. (1990): Positive effects and limitations of client-centred therapy with schizophrenic patients. In G. Lietaer, J. Rombauts, and R. Van Balen (eds): *Client-Centered and Experiential Psychotherapy in the Nineties* (pp. 637–44). Leuven: Leuven University Press.

Teusch, L., Beyerle, U., Lange, H. U., Schenck, G. K. and Stadtmüller, G. (1983): The client-centred approach to schizophrenic patients: First empirical results. In W. R. Minsel and W. Herff (eds.): *Research in Psychotherapeutic Approaches* (pp. 140–8). Frankfurt: Peter Lang.

Thorgaard, L. and Rosenbaum, B. (1996): Tidlig og Vedholdende Intervention ved Schizofreni. Unpublished paper.

Van Werde, D. (1994a): An introduction to client-centred pre-therapy. In D. Mearns (1994): *Developing Person-Centred Counselling* (pp. 121–5). London: Sage.

Van Werde, D. (1994b): Dealing with the possibility of psychotic content in a seemingly congruent communication. In D. Mearns (1994): *Developing Person-Centred Counselling* (pp. 125–8). London: Sage.

Van Werde, D. (1998): Anchorage as a core concept in working with psychotic people. In B. Thorne and E. Lambers (eds): *Person-Centred Therapy: A European Perspective* (pp. 195–205). London: Sage.

Van Werde, D. and Morton, I. (1999): The relevance of Prouty's pre-therapy to dementia care. In I. Morton (1999): *Person-Centred Approaches to Dementia Care*. Oxon: Winslow Press.

Warner, M. S. (1991): Fragile process. In L. Fusek (ed): *New Directions in Client-Centred Therapy: Practice with Difficult Client Populations* (pp. 41–58). Chicago: Chicago Counseling and Psychotherapy Research Center.

Winnicot, D. W. (1987): *The Maturational Processes and the Facilitating Environment*. London: Hogarth.

INDEX

PCCS Books

The largest list of Client-Centred Therapy and Person-Centred Approach books in the world

Client-Centred Therapy and the Person-Centred Approach
Essential Readers
Series edited by Tony Merry

Client-Centred Therapy: A revolutionary paradigm
Jerold Bozarth

Experiences in Relatedness: Groupwork and the person-centred approach
Colin Lago & Mhairi MacMillan (Eds)

Women Writing in the Person-Centred Approach
Irene Fairhurst (Ed)

Understanding Psychotherapy: Fifty years of client-centred theory and practice
C.H. Patterson

The Person-Centred Approach: A passionate presence
Peggy Natiello

Family, Self and Psychotherapy: A person-centred perspective
Ned L. Gaylin

Contributions to Client-Centered Therapy and the Person-Centered Approach
Nathaniel J. Raskin

Rogers' Therapeutic Conditions: Evolution, Theory and Practice
Series edited by Gill Wyatt

Volume 1: Congruence
Gill Wyatt (Ed)

Volume 2: Empathy
Sheila Haugh & Tony Merry (Eds)

Volume 3: Unconditional Positive Regard
Jerold Bozarth & Paul Wilkins (Eds)

Volume 4: Contact and Perception
Gill Wyatt & Pete Sanders (Eds)